GREAT ART IDEAS FOR KIDS K-3

Gail Tuchman

Troll Associates

Interior Illustrations by: Ethel Gold

ISBN: 0-8167-2595-0

Printed in the United States of America.

10 9 8 7 6 5 4

CONTENTS

INTRODUCTION

With this book, children will turn newspapers into log cabins, tin cans into zoo animals, peanuts into puppets, and pine cones into turkeys. Common inexpensive and natural materials—from paper to pine cones—are transformed into art.

Great Art Ideas for Kids K–3 offers you a wide range of hands-on art activities to share with your class, all of which will help to develop children's awareness of their own creative capabilities. The ideas will challenge children and encourage them to strengthen their skills.

These activities are arranged from September through the summer. Some projects offer ideas for holidays and seasonal activities. Others can be used at any time, in conjunction with lessons being taught. (For example, children might use the origami wallets they create for math lessons involving money.) For each month, two Activity Sheets are included. These are addressed to children and include all the information they need to do fun independent projects. Teachers can simply photocopy Activity Sheets and distribute them to children.

Each project lists the materials you'll need and provides simple instructions. The step-by-step instructions are directly transferable to the child for a ready-made art lesson. Before you begin a project, read through the directions, gather all materials, and set aside a block of time. You might call in parents, older students, or other volunteers to help children with projects, as needed.

Children will learn a variety of different art techniques: paper folding, papier-mâché, painting, printing, puppetry, nature crafts, rubbings, weaving, batik, sewing, crayoning, casting. They'll also explore many media: clay, paper, paints, crayons, cans, boxes, various other household materials, and materials from nature. Although the projects yield specific products, the process will open the way to using the techniques and materials for other kinds of artwork in the future.

The ideas will tap the children's imagination and interest and provide them with basic techniques that they can use whenever they have the impulse to create art. After learning a technique, children should be encouraged to experiment with it, and to create all sorts of variations. As children learn to manipulate new materials, their own natural ingenuity will be awakened, resulting in ideas for original designs and objects.

The projects emphasize recycling and reusing materials, such as bags, boxes, metal cans, cardboard tubes, glass jars, magazines, and scraps of string, felt, and yarn. Consider setting up a classroom "recycling" area. Encourage children to bring in materials that can be recycled into art projects and sort them into cartons. Whenever a project calls for these objects, they'll be right at hand. Ask your principal to request recycled paper when ordering school supplies.

Check all arts-and-crafts materials to make sure they do not present any health hazards for children by ingestion, inhalation, or skin contact. Always use water-based markers, glues, and paints, and talc-free, premixed clays. Never use solvent-based adhesives like rubber cement, or solvents like shellac. Use watercolor, liquid tempera, or acrylic paints. Make sure that paints do not contain toxic pigments, such as cadmiums and vermillions.

Inhaling dusts and powders from dry clay and plaster can be hazardous to children. Yet such projects as casting may be done by children if the steps that are potentially hazardous are removed. For example, you can mix plaster or powdered tempera with water in a well-ventilated area when children are not present. Plaster casting should never be done of body parts, because the plaster can cause severe burns.

The Labeling of Hazardous Art Materials Act, a United States law, requires that warning labels appear on art materials with chronic hazards as well as acute hazards. Such materials are inappropriate for children to use. There is a list available of publications about art hazards and safety precautions for elementary school children. To obtain this list, send a self-addressed stamped envelope to: Center for Safety in the Arts, 5 Beekman Street, New York, NY 10038.

The projects in *Great Art Ideas for Kids K–3* are enjoyable for teachers and children alike. Each project leads to improvisation with various materials and art techniques, and this improvisation is sure to result in many new, exciting projects.

Grateful acknowledgment to Barbara Packer for permission to use many of the ideas we created together.

Self-Portraits

What You Need

brown wrapping paper
pencil or black crayon
scissors
tempera and paintbrushes
masking tape

What You Do

1. Have children work with partners. Place a sheet of large brown wrapping paper on the floor. One child lies on his or her back on the paper with arms extended slightly outward and palms down. The second child traces the first child's outline on the paper. Then the children switch roles to make a tracing of the second child.

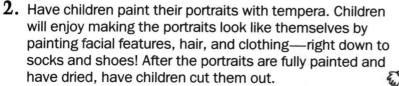

2. Have children paint their portraits with tempera. Children will enjoy making the portraits look like themselves by painting facial features, hair, and clothing—right down to socks and shoes! After the portraits are fully painted and have dried, have children cut them out.

3. Create a "Circle of Back-to-School Friends" around the classroom by hanging the self-portraits next to one another with hands joined. Use rolled-up pieces of masking tape to hold the hands of the self-portraits.

4. Children can tape or paint their names onto the portraits.

5. Use this "Circle of Friends" to encourage children to connect with old friends and get acquainted with new ones.

SEPTEMBER
Silhouettes

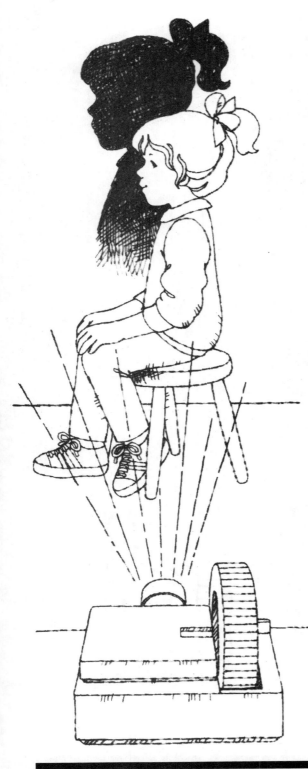

What You Need

projector
black construction paper
masking tape
white crayon
scissors
white glue
white construction paper

What You Do

1. Explain to children that a silhouette is an outline of something or someone, especially in profile. Tell them it is usually a dark shape against a light background.

2. Shine the light from a projector onto a blank classroom wall. Ask a child to sit in the "limelight" (in front of the light) with the light shining on the side of his or her face. A profile will project onto the wall directly behind the child.

3. Have another child tape a sheet of black construction paper to the wall, directly over the profile. Using a *white* crayon, the child should then trace the projected child's profile onto the paper.

4. After their profiles are traced, have children cut out the black silhouettes and glue them onto large sheets of white construction paper.

5. Create silhouettes of other things. Move a desk in front of the projector light. Try putting different objects, such as a plant, a book, or a stuffed animal, in front of the light. Trace the outlines of these objects in the same way, cut them out, and glue them onto white paper.

6. Encourage children to make silhouettes of family members at home, bring them to school, and "introduce" them to the class.

Box Model Neighborhood

What You Need

boxes (various sizes and shapes)
juice and milk cartons—pint (500 ml), quart (1 liter),
    1/2 gallon (2 liters)
brown wrapping paper
scissors
white glue
tape
construction paper in different colors
tempera and paintbrushes

What You Do

1. Plan out a model representation of the neighborhood by discussing the sizes and shapes of the school and surrounding buildings. Then match the sizes and shapes of boxes to these buildings. For example, a pint (500-ml) juice container might be a one-story house, a quart (1-liter) container an apartment house, a few attached half-gallon (2-liter) containers a skyscraper, a shoe box a row of stores, and a cylindrical oatmeal box a modern museum or a silo.

2. Cover each box model with brown wrapping paper.

3. Cut into the boxes to create windows and doors. One side of the windows and doors can be left attached so they swing open. Or cut doors and windows from construction paper and glue them onto the boxes. They can also be painted on. Add other building parts, such as chimneys, by cutting, gluing, taping, or painting.

4. Paint the rest of the building with tempera.

5. Arrange the models on a large sheet of brown wrapping paper to re-create the actual blocks around the school. Draw lines to represent streets.

6. The Box Model Neighborhood can grow and change during the year as new buildings are put up or old ones torn down. Other blocks in the neighborhood might be added to the model.

Nature Rubbings

Leaf Collage Rubbing and Multinature Collage Rubbing

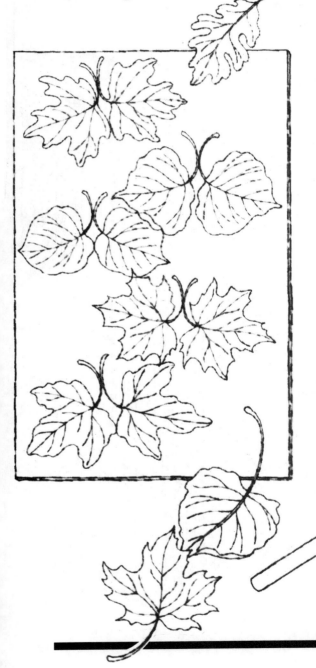

What You Do

1. To make a rubbing of a leaf, first glue the leaf, vein side facing up, onto cardboard or construction paper.

2. Place a sheet of thin paper on top of the leaf and rub with the side of an unwrapped crayon. Hold the paper down firmly while rubbing, so it doesn't slip. Work on a small section at a time, making even strokes and moving the crayon in the same direction: from top to bottom, from left to right, from the middle outward, or from the edges inward.

3. Tell children they are "lifting" the design from the leaf's surface. As they rub, they'll see the image of the leaf appear on the paper. Explain that a rubbing is a print taken from any surface that is raised, indented, or has texture.

4. Before removing the paper, make sure the design is finished. If not, rub some more.

Leaf Collage Rubbing

1. Make a collage of all different varieties, shapes, and sizes of leaves. Arrange the leaves in an interesting pattern on cardboard or construction paper. Leaves might be cut in half to fit certain spaces or arranged to take on special shapes—such as a butterfly's shape.

2. Once the leaves are arranged, glue them down. Let the glue dry. Then make a rubbing of the collage. Using autumn colors, make leaves shades of green, brown, yellow, red, and orange. Experiment with two-tone leaves by rubbing one part of a leaf with one color crayon and another part with a second color.

Multinature Collage Rubbing

1. Make a collage of assorted objects from nature: twigs, pebbles, ferns, feathers, tree bark, and so on, combining many textures. Then take a rubbing of the collage. (*Note:* when working with hard-to-secure objects like pebbles and twigs, tape the underside of the object to cardboard, instead of gluing.)

2. Vary the effect by experimenting with different shades of paper and crayons. You can even try dark paper with white crayons. The design possibilities are endless! Remember always to use *thin* paper to do your rubbing to let the impressions of natural objects come through.

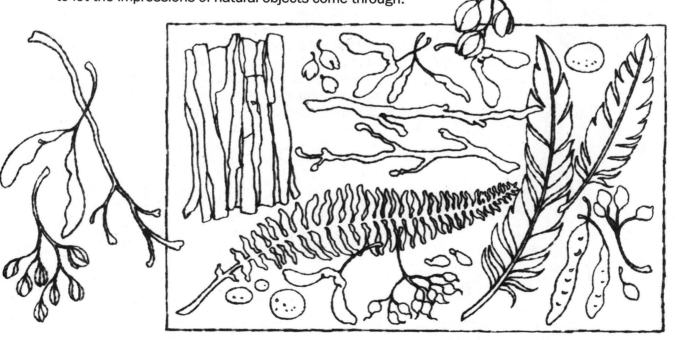

Vegetable Prints

Book Covers and Homework Pads

What You Need

vegetables (such as carrot, potato, turnip, onion, cabbage)

knife *for teacher*

string (for tying cabbage)

tempera and paintbrushes

flat tray or dish (for spreading paint)

large sheet of white paper (for book cover)

typewriter or computer paper

stapler

What You Do

1. Vegetables can be carved into simple shapes and used to print repeating designs. Cut vegetables (carrot, potato, turnip, onion, cabbage) in half. If using cabbage, tie it loosely with string to keep the leaves from separating. Let vegetables air-dry for several hours so their juices won't interfere with printing. The open side will become the printing surface.

2. Draw a simple shape (triangle, rectangle, circle, or free-form) on the surface. Cut away the background, leaving the shape raised.

3. Brush the vegetable (except for the cabbage) with a thin coat of paint. Then press it firmly onto a sheet of typewriter or computer paper to make a print. If using a cabbage, press it into a tray of paint and then onto the paper, rolling or wiggling it slightly.

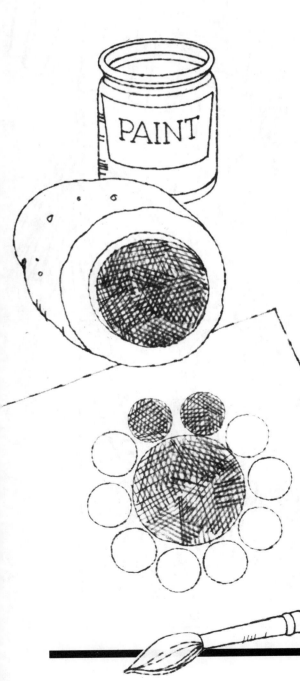

4. Have children experiment with the amount of paint they need to apply and the pressure they need when stamping.

5. Explore different possibilities in printing patterns. Print one vegetable pattern over and over in the same or different colors. Try a variety of vegetables and overlap some shapes and colors. Print a picture, such as a flower.

Vegetable Print Book Covers

1. Print repeated patterns on a large sheet of white paper, and let it dry. This will be the book cover.

2. Place the vegetable-printed side of the book cover facedown.

3. Place an open book in the center of the book cover.

4. Fold over the top and bottom sections as shown.

5. Remove the book and place it on the cover. Fold the side sections of the cover over the inside of the book.

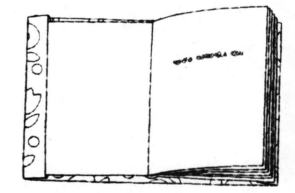

6. Slip book into folded side pockets of the book cover.

Vegetable Print Homework Pads

1. Fold typewriter or computer paper in half horizontally and cut along fold. Each paper will provide two pages for the memo pad. Cut as many sheets as desired.

2. Stamp vegetable prints on the upper or lower portion of each page. If you are working with a carrot, try printing a border. Leave enough open space to write homework assignments.

3. When prints dry, staple together the pages of the homework pad(s).

Dried Wildflower Decorations

Bring a little of the outdoors into the classroom with a dried wildflower decoration!

What You Need

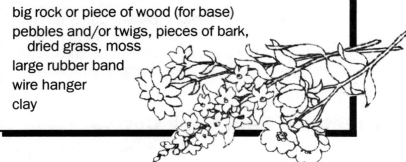

bunch of wildflowers
big rock or piece of wood (for base)
pebbles and/or twigs, pieces of bark, dried grass, moss
large rubber band
wire hanger
clay

What You Do

1. Group together about a dozen wildflowers. Attach them to a wire hanger with a rubber band. Then hang the flowers upside down to dry. It takes from one to two weeks for them to dry.

2. Wash the wood, rock, pebbles, twigs, and pieces of bark. Let them air-dry thoroughly.

3. Use the big rock or piece of wood as the base. Press a few small balls of clay onto it. Stick the wildflowers into the clay. Try different arrangements. Decide what looks best by moving flowers, adding them, or taking them away. You may need to adjust the lengths of the stems by cutting them. Use more or less clay as needed.

4. Once you're happy with your arrangement, cover the rest of the clay. Press pebbles, bark, dried grass, moss, or even broken-up twigs into it.

14

Pasta Pencil Case

*You can turn an empty spaghetti box into a pencil case—with the pasta on the **outside**!*

What You Need

uncooked pasta (different kinds)
bright tempera and paintbrushes
empty spaghetti box (8-ounce [226.8 grams] size)
white glue

What You Do

1. Pasta comes in different colors. Red pasta gets its color from tomatoes. Spinach gives pasta a green color. Paint plain pasta with your own special colors. Use a thick coat of tempera. If the pasta is shaped like a tube or a bow tie, first paint one side and let it dry. Then paint the other. Some other kinds of pasta should also be painted in two steps.

2. Place the spaghetti box on one of its sides. Spread some glue on it. Arrange the pasta shapes into a design. Stick them onto the side of the box. Cover the entire side. Allow it to dry about twenty minutes.

3. Turn the box on another side. Glue the pasta in the same way. Continue until all four sides and the top are covered and have dried.

4. Pencils will look real *sharp* in your pasta pencil case! Keep it in your desk at school, or keep it at home for doing homework. Don't carry it around in your school bag—the pasta might break off.

15

Leaf Prints

OCTOBER

Lunch Bags

What You Need

fresh green leaves (different types and sizes)
tempera and paintbrushes
sheet of newspaper (to work on)
tray or shallow dish (for spreading paint)
construction paper
sheets of scrap paper
brown paper lunch bags

What You Do

1. Try either of these methods to make leaf prints.
   Dipping the leaf. Pour some paint into a tray or shallow dish and spread it out. Dip the vein side of the leaf into the paint and press it flat against the tray.
   Painting the leaf. Place a leaf, vein side up, on a sheet of newspaper. Paint the vein side with a thick coat of tempera, straight from the jar.

2. Place the leaf, paint side down, on a sheet of construction paper. Cover it with a piece of scrap paper. Press down on the scrap paper, and rub across it with your fist *without* letting the leaf move.

3. Remove the scrap paper and lift off the leaf.

4. Practice making more leaf prints in the same way. Try printing different types of leaves together to make designs.

Leaf-Print Lunch Bags

When children feel comfortable with the technique and are happy with their designs, they can decorate lunch bags with leaf-print patterns.

1. Have children place the lunch bag down flat and print on it.

2. Have children put their names on the bags, and then let them take the bags home to be filled.

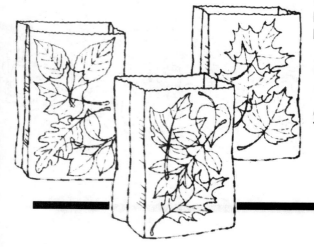

What You Need

Cloth Ghost
newspaper
pieces of old sheets or pillow cases
string
tempera and paintbrush, or markers

Tissue Ghost
tissues
string or rubber band
markers
paper clip

Ghosts! Ghosts! Ghosts!

Cloth Ghosts and Tissue Ghosts

What You Do
Cloth Ghost

1. Crumple up a sheet of newspaper into a ball for the ghost's head.

2. Drape an appropriate-size piece of white cloth over the newspaper, so that it covers the ghost's head and hangs down to form the body.

3. Tie the cloth securely with string just below the head.

4. Use paint or markers to add eyes, a nose, and a mouth.

5. Hang the ghost from a piece of string. Fasten it to the back of the string already around the ghost's neck.

Tissue Ghost

1. Wad up a tissue so that it forms a ball.

2. Insert the ball into the center of another tissue.

3. Gather the second tissue around the tissue ball and tie it with a string or secure it with a rubber band. This separates the ghost's head from the body. Fluff out the body tissue with your hand.

4. Use a marker to add ghostly facial features.

5. To hang up the ghost in the classroom, bend open the center of a paper clip, leaving the "hook" at each end. Insert one end of the clip into the rubber band or string at the back of the ghost's head. Hang the ghost from the hook at the other end.

Spooky Pictures

**Crayon Ghosts,
Crayon Ghost Rubbing,
Ghostly Candle Painting**

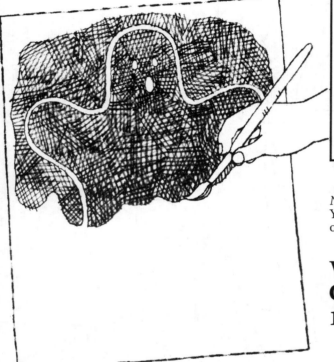

What You Need

Crayon Ghosts
white drawing paper
white crayon
watercolors and paintbrushes

Crayon Ghost Rubbing
objects for rubbing
thin white paper (typewriter, computer, or
   rice paper)
white crayon, unwrapped
tape or glue
cardboard or construction paper
watercolors and paintbrushes

Ghostly Candle Painting
white candle
other materials, same as those used for
   Crayon Ghosts

Note: These three projects are variations of the wax-resist technique. You might offer a choice and have different groups of children work on these projects simultaneously.

What You Do
Crayon Ghosts

1. Draw pictures of ghosts or goblins on *white* drawing paper using a *white* crayon. By working with white-on-white, the completed pictures will be almost invisible, like a ghost!

2. Have children exchange drawings with classmates. They should use one color of watercolor to paint over the entire surface of the drawing. The crayon ghosts will magically appear! The paint "rolls off," or resists the crayon wax to bring the ghosts into full view.

Crayon Ghost Rubbing

1. Suggest that each child find an object with an interesting surface and then make a rubbing. Have children use thin *white* paper and an unwrapped *white* crayon. The object chosen should be kept secret. (If necessary, refer to pages 10–11 for directions on rubbings.)

2. Tell children to swap rubbings with classmates. They should use watercolor to paint lightly over the rubbing, always moving the brush in the same direction. The ghost rubbing will appear like magic!

Ghostly Candle Painting

1. Use a *white* candle on *white* drawing paper to draw a spooky object: a haunted house, a witch, and so on. Press down hard when drawing with the candle. The picture will appear almost invisible.

2. Use watercolor to bring out the ghostly picture. Candle wax resists paint just as crayon wax does.

19

Papier-Mâché Halloween Masks

What You Need

round 9-inch (23-cm) balloons
   (one balloon makes two masks)*
liquid starch, or flour and water
bowl (if using flour and water)
tray (in which to soak paper)
newspaper
paper towels
pin *for teacher*
sharp knife *for teacher*
tempera and paintbrushes
string

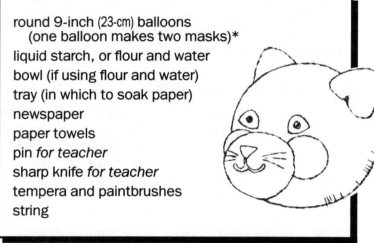

Safety Note: Teacher or another adult should blow up the balloons. Swallowing deflated balloons can be dangerous.

What You Do

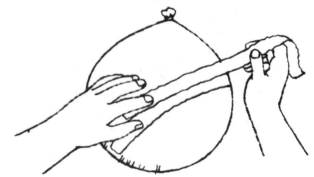

1. Explain to children that papier-mâché is a method of building up layers of paper strips soaked in a paste-water solution to create anything from bowls to toys to masks. It's easy to mold and is strong when it dries.

2. Teacher or another adult should blow up the balloons and knot the ends.

3. Have children work in pairs to cover one balloon. Pour some liquid starch into a tray. (Or mix flour and water in a bowl to make a smooth paste. This paste may be used instead of liquid starch for making masks.)

4. Tear newspaper pages into strips approximately 3/4 inch (2 cm) wide and 3 inches (7 1/2 cm) long. (Children don't have to follow these exact measurements; use them as a guide so that strips aren't too wide or too long.) Put a strip into the tray, soaking it completely in the starch.

5. Place the soaked paper strip on the balloon and press it down. Then wet another piece and put it on the balloon next to the first piece, so that they overlap slightly.

6. Add soaked strips, one by one, all around the balloon, until it is covered. To make the mask stronger, build up three more layers of strips around the balloon. Have children smooth out any lumpy paste with their fingers.

7. Soak a paper towel in the starch and add it to the balloon. Continue adding soaked towels until two layers cover the balloon. Smooth down the towels.

8. Let the balloon dry for about five days. Hang it by its knot to dry or turn it each day so that it dries evenly on all sides.

9. Teacher or another adult should pop the balloon with a pin when the paper is dry, then cut the thick paper ball in half with a sharp knife. There are two masks, one for each child in the pair.

10. Design the masks by painting them or by building up the features with more papier-mâché strips.

11. Here's how to build up the masks: Soak more newspaper strips in starch. Add small pieces of soaked newspaper to the areas to be built up—eyes, nose, mouth, ears. Roll soaked paper strips to make shapes for eyebrows, lips, and so on. Press down the paper while working, so that it sticks to the surface.

12. After the features are created, add a layer or two of soaked paper-towel pieces over the built-up areas, keeping the same shape. This is done to hold the features in place and to make the mask's surface smooth.

13. Let the masks dry, and then paint them with tempera. Hang the masks for Halloween.

14. Use the same technique to create papier-mâché masks of historical figures and storybook characters during the school year.

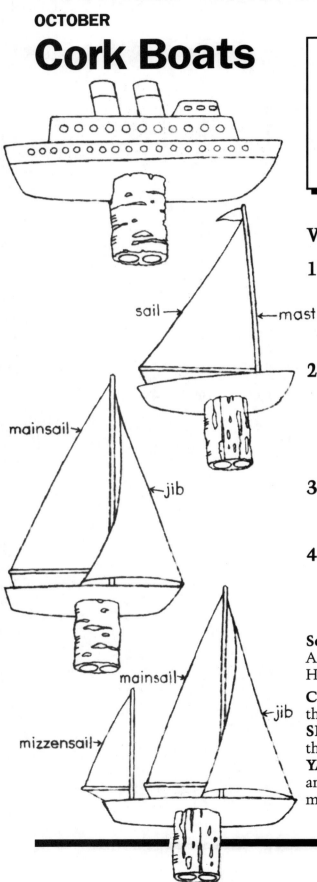

OCTOBER
Cork Boats

sail → ← mast

mainsail →

← jib

mainsail →

← jib

mizzensail →

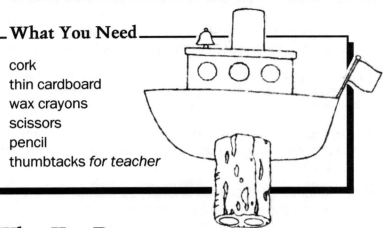

What You Need

cork
thin cardboard
wax crayons
scissors
pencil
thumbtacks *for teacher*

What You Do

1. Cork boats to represent the Niña, the Pinta, and the Santa María can be made for Columbus Day. Pilgrim ships can be created for Thanksgiving. Many types of boats can be made to enhance the study of water transportation.

2. Draw the outline of a boat on a sheet of cardboard. Consider its size in relationship to the cork—the cork will hold up the boat and float it. Cut out the entire boat as one piece. Use crayons to color it. Since the crayon wax acts as a seal to waterproof the boat, tell children to color every part heavily, including the edges.

3. Draw a pencil line across the exact center of the cork. Teacher or another adult should use a blade to make a slit 1/4 inch (1/2 cm) deep along the line.

4. Insert the boat into the cork. To keep the vessel from toppling over when it's in the water, teacher should push two thumbtacks into the bottom of the cork, a little bit apart from each other. Boats can be set afloat in water.

Setting Sail

A whole fleet of cork boats may be created in the same way. Here are some popular sailboats:

CATBOAT Sailboat with a single mast set well forward in the bow and one sail.
SLOOP Sailboat with a single mast toward the middle of the boat and two sails (a mainsail and a jib).
YAWL Sailboat with two masts (mainmast placed forward and a smaller mast placed astern) and at least three sails (a mainsail, a jib, and a mizzensail).

What You Need

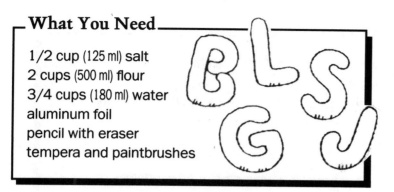

1/2 cup (125 ml) salt
2 cups (500 ml) flour
3/4 cups (180 ml) water
aluminum foil
pencil with eraser
tempera and paintbrushes

Safety Note: Teacher or another adult should preheat oven to 325°F (160°C). Do *not* do the baking part of this project by yourself. Ask an adult to help you.

What You Do

1. To make the dough, mix together the salt and flour. Add the water slowly. *Knead,* press and squeeze, the mixture for about five minutes.

2. Roll and knead a lump of dough into a smooth, round ball. It should be about the size of a tennis ball. Place the ball on a piece of foil.

3. Use the tips of your fingers to flatten the ball. It should look like a dinner plate. If you need to, smooth the flat dough with a damp cloth.

4. Break off small pieces of the leftover dough. Roll them into marble-sized balls. Make one dough ball for each letter of your first name.

5. Roll the ball between your hands until it looks like a worm.

6. Use this worm-shaped dough to make the first letter of your name. To make some letters, you may need to use more than one piece of dough.

7. Shape all the letters of your name. Press them gently across the center of your plate. Decorate the plate by using the leftover dough.

8. Make a hole at the top and bottom of your plate with the eraser end of a pencil.

9. Ask your teacher or another adult to put the plate (on the foil) in the oven. Bake for one hour. An adult should remove the dough plate from the oven. Let it cool.

10. Paint the plate with tempera, and allow it to dry.

11. Your nameplate is ready for hanging.

Nameplates

Here's a recipe for clay that you can make and bake into your own nameplate.

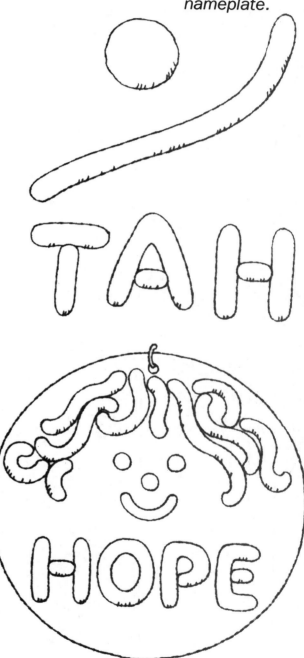

Window Paintings

*Paint Halloween pictures
right on your classroom windows!*

What You Need

white powdered kitchen cleanser
water
paper cups or small containers (for paint mixture)
wooden stick (for stirring)
tempera
cotton swabs or paintbrushes
rag or towel (for wiping paint off windows)

What You Do

1. Have your teacher shake some white powdered kitchen cleanser into a cup. Add a little water. Stir the mixture to make a thick paste. This mixture will be your "window paint." It will have a chalky white look—for painting spooks on Halloween!

2. If you like, you can put color into the window paint. Make a few other cups of the mixture. Add a different color of tempera to each cup. Stir well.

3. Dip a cotton swab (or paintbrush) into the window paint. Use it to paint Halloween pictures on your classroom windows. Work with your classmates to cover the windows with webs, witches, ghosts, goblins, jack-o'-lanterns, and haunted houses.

4. You can surprise trick-or-treaters at home by creating these spooky window paintings.

5. After Halloween, just wipe the windows clean with a damp rag or towel.

Tin Can Picture Frames

What You Need

empty, shallow tin cans: round, oval, or rectangular, with tops removed (salmon cans, tuna cans, sardine cans)
Note: Do not use pop-top or deep cans.

scissors

glue

masking tape

materials to decorate cans: acrylic paints and paintbrushes; adhesive-backed paper, scraps of colorful construction or tissue paper, wrapping paper, and foil paper; scraps of sequins, yarn, and buttons; seeds, pebbles, twigs, small dried flowers, and other natural knickknacks

photograph or picture (artwork) to be framed (measured and cut to fit into base of can)

ribbon (for hanging)

What You Do

1. Tell children that they can turn tin cans into frames for special photographs and pictures.

2. Prepare cans by peeling or soaking off paper wrappings. Clean each can thoroughly with soap and water. Dry the cans.

3. Explain to children that their pictures will later be added to the inner flat bottom of the can. They should keep that in mind when planning their decorations.

4. Decorate the can by using materials suggested above. Here are some ideas:

   ● Paint a can inside and out with acrylic paints. Add a border of lace around the rim of the can. Cut lace pieces and glue to the sides.

   ● Cut and glue paper petals to the can to make a flower frame.

5. Glue a photograph or other picture to the inside base of the can.

6. A long ribbon, glued or taped to the back of the can and looped at the top, acts as a hanger for the tin can frame. Or the frame can stand on its side with the picture upright, if the particular decoration does not interfere with the can's ability to stand.

Corn Husk Dolls

What You Need

14 corn husks, dried (see step 2 for drying instructions)

corn silk, dried (see step 2 for drying instructions)

newspaper (to work on)

thin string

scissors

straight pins *for teacher*

glue

felt-tip pens

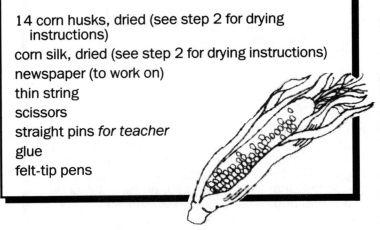

What You Do

1. Tell children that dolls fashioned from dried corn husks originated with Native Americans, who passed their technique on to early settlers. These traditional dolls are part of the United States' native heritage.

2. Peel off individual husks from the corn, layer by layer. Spread the largest husks on newspaper and allow them to dry until the green bleaches out to a pale tan color. Allow the corn silk to dry on newspaper as well. Drying takes at least a week.

3. Soak the dried husks in water until they are soft enough to work with. Shake off the excess water and place the husks on newspaper.

4. Gather eight of the husks together and tie them tightly with string at the wide end.

5. Fold each husk down over the tied end, pulling firmly, until the tied part is covered by four husks on each side.

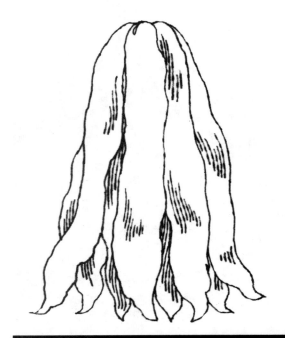

6. Tie the husks tightly together about 1 1/2 inches (4 cm) down from the top to form the head and neck.

7. Now use three additional husks to make the arms. Tie the three husks together with string at one end, braid them, and tie at the other end. Trim the ends slightly so that the "hands" are even.

8. Separate the body husks so that there are four husks in front and four in back. Insert the braided arms crosswise between the two sections. Tie the doll at the waist.

9. Fold two additional husks in half vertically. Place the center of a husk over each shoulder. Cross them over the front and back of the body, making certain that they lie flat and untwisted. Tie them at the waist with string. Fold another husk in half, wrap it around the waist, and secure it with string.

10. To form legs, separate the husks so there are four husks on each side of the body. Tie each cluster of four about 1 inch (2 1/2 cm) from the bottom. Trim the edges slightly to make the "feet" even.

11. To prevent the arms from standing straight out when the husks dry, bend them into a more natural position. Teacher should secure them temporarily with pins. Remove the pins when the doll dries.

12. Wet the dried corn silk. Arrange the silk in any hair style—braided, twisted, flowing, or cut short. Glue the silk onto the head for hair.

13. When the husks dry, use felt-tip pens to draw the eyes, nose, and mouth.

Box Lid Serving Tray

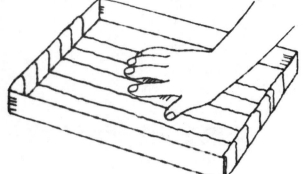

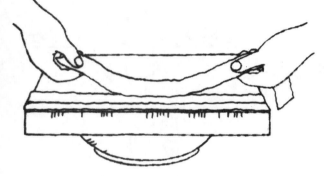

What You Need

box lid (from shoe box or
   sturdy cardboard gift box)

flour and water, or liquid starch

2 bowls (one for mixing,
   one to use as a stand)

large spoon (for stirring)

newspaper

acrylic paints and paintbrushes (Note: tempera
   may be used if acrylic gloss medium and varnish
   is not applied.)

acrylic gloss medium and varnish and brush *for
   teacher* (optional)

What You Do

1. Tell children that they are going to use papier-mâché to make serving trays out of box lids.

2. Mix flour and water in a bowl to make a smooth paste. (Put 1 cup (250 ml) flour into the bowl. Add water slowly, mixing until the flour-water mixture is creamy and thick.) Or use liquid starch.

3. Tear newspaper sheets into strips about 1 inch (2 1/2 cm) wide and three inches (8 cm) long.

4. Dip a strip into the bowl. Rub off excess by pulling the strip out over the side of the bowl. Place the paper strip onto the inside of the box lid and press it down. Add another strip of newspaper in the same way, so that it slightly overlaps the first strip. Continue adding paste-dipped newspaper strips, one by one, all around the lid until it is covered.

5. Turn the lid over and cover the top and sides in the same way. To strengthen the lid so that it will make a sturdy serving tray, build up two more layers of newspaper strips on the inside and outside. Have children smooth out any lumpy paste with their fingers.

6. Allow the lid tray to dry for about five days, turning it each day so that it dries evenly on both sides. When the tray is dry, paint it with acrylic paints.

7. To protect the painted surface, teacher may cover the tray with a coat of acrylic gloss medium and varnish. Let the tray dry overnight.

Peanut Shell Puppets

What You Need

large, fat peanut shells

felt-tip pens or fine-line markers

white glue

material for hair (optional; bits of yarn, cotton ball)

material for clothing (optional; pieces of cloth or felt)

thin piece of material to cover fingers (optional)

What You Do

1. Tell children that puppets can be made from a variety of materials—from peanut shells to clothespins. The puppets can be used for acting out original class plays, favorite stories, historical events, or holiday celebrations. Puppet shows can be staged right on a desk with a cloth draped over the top.

2. To make peanut shell finger puppets, poke out or break off one end of the peanut shell and remove the peanut. Have children stick their fingers inside the empty shells to make sure the shells are large enough. If the fit is too tight, have them "try on" other peanut shells.

3. Have children use felt-tip pens or fine-line markers to draw a face at the top of the peanut shell. Glue on bits of yarn or cotton for the hair. Add a little felt hat, if desired.

4. If the peanut shell is long enough, have children make a little face near the top with markers and draw peanut arms and clothing. Small pieces of cloth can be glued on to create peanut puppet clothes.

5. If children make only one puppet, they can drape a thin piece of material over the rest of their hand. Or they can make a peanut shell puppet for each finger.

Paper Finger Puppets

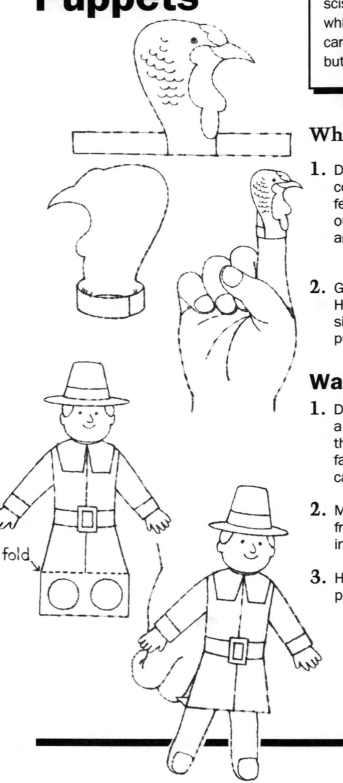

What You Need

construction paper
crayons
scissors
white glue
cardboard
buttons for eyes and yarn for hair (optional)

What You Do

1. Draw the head and neck of a person or animal on construction paper. Use crayons to color the facial features and hair. Draw 3/4-inch (2-cm) "tabs" extending out from both sides of the neck (as shown). Cut the head and tabs out as one piece.

2. Glue the tabs into a ring that fits around the fingertip. Have children sit the puppets on their fingers. They simply bend or wiggle their fingers to make the puppets move.

Walking Finger Puppets

1. Draw a figure on cardboard or construction paper. Leave a 1-inch (2 1/2-cm) extension tab at the bottom. Cut out the figure and tab as one piece. Use crayons to color facial features, hair, and clothing. If the figure is cardboard, button eyes and yarn hair can be glued on.

2. Make a horizontal fold line to separate the extension tab from the body. Cut out two holes large enough for the index and middle fingers.

3. Have children slip their fingers through the holes to make puppet legs that walk, run, or hop about.

fold

What You Need

wooden forked-type clothespins (Do not use clamp-type.)

tempera and paintbrushes, felt-tip pens, or fine-line markers

scraps of fabric, yarn (optional)

white glue

pipe cleaners

wooden craft sticks

masking tape

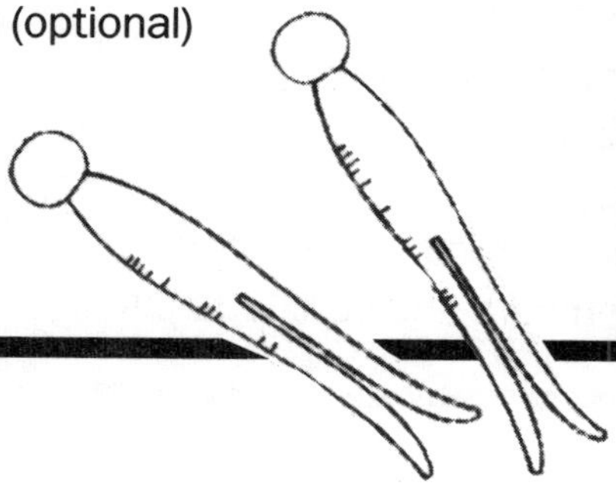

Clothespin Puppets

What You Do

1. Use tempera, felt-tip pens, or fine-line markers to make a face on the rounded part of a clothespin. This part will be the puppet's head.

2. Paint or color hair and clothing on the clothespin. Pieces of yarn and scraps of fabric can be glued on as well. Add details to both the front and the back of the clothespin.

3. Twist a pipe cleaner around the "neck" to create arms. Bend them up, down, out, or across the body.

4. Tape together two or three wooden craft sticks to form one long stick. Dab a little glue on the end of the top stick, or stick on a rolled-up piece of masking tape (sticky sides out).

5. Insert the stick between the forks of the clothespin so that it sticks to the inner part of the rounded top. Use the stick to move the clothespin puppet.

Gourd Rattles

Long ago, gourds were dried and used by Native Americans as rattles. Gourd rattles are still used today.

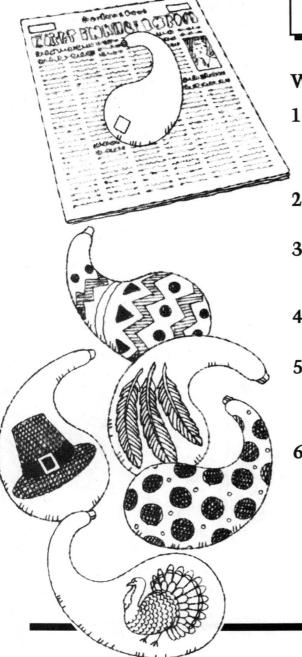

What You Need

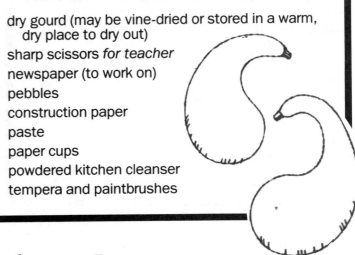

dry gourd (may be vine-dried or stored in a warm, dry place to dry out)

sharp scissors *for teacher*

newspaper (to work on)

pebbles

construction paper

paste

paper cups

powdered kitchen cleanser

tempera and paintbrushes

What You Do

1. Choose a gourd. Look for one that is shaped like a rattle. It should have a curved neck. Try holding onto the end and shaking it. Is the gourd large enough to work with? Does it feel comfortable in your hand?

2. Dry the gourd. Then soak the dried gourd in water for 24 hours.

3. Ask your teacher or another adult to use scissors to make a hole in the gourd. The hole should be large enough for the seeds to come out.

4. Spread out the newspaper. Shake the gourd over the newspaper until all the seeds fall out.

5. Put a handful of pebbles into the gourd. Cut a patch of construction paper large enough to cover the hole. Dip the paper patch in paste. Then use it to seal the hole. Let the paste dry.

6. Let the gourd dry completely. Then set up a paper cup for each color of paint you want to use. In each cup, have your teacher mix a small amount of powdered kitchen cleanser with your tempera. This mixture will help the paint stick to the gourd. Paint a picture or design onto your gourd. You may want to decorate the gourd for Thanksgiving.

Shake your rattle in time to music while you sing or dance. Have a "gourd" time!

What You Need

6 sheets of construction paper (different colors)
pencil
scissors
crayons
white glue
pine cone
pieces of fabric (optional)

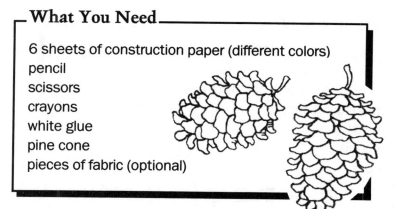

Pine Cone Turkey Place Cards

Decorate your desk at school with a pine cone turkey place card. Then bring your place card home to put on the table at Thanksgiving dinner. You might enjoy making place cards for other members of your family.

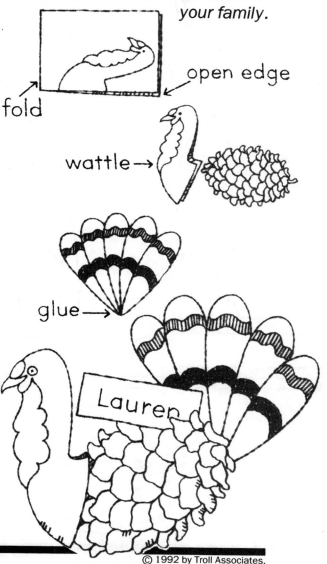

What You Do

1. Fold a sheet of construction paper in half. Draw the turkey's head on the paper. Position the head as shown. Make sure the head is a good size for the turkey body (pine cone) you have selected. Keeping the paper folded, cut out the head. You now have a paired piece.

2. Use crayons to draw eyes and the turkey's wattle. Or you can glue on sequins for the eyes and pieces of paper or fabric for the wattle.

3. Glue the two paper heads together at the top, leaving the bottom of the neck open (unglued).

4. Place your pine cone on its side. Glue the open ends of the neck onto the tip end of the cone.

5. Now make the turkey's tail feathers. Choose different colors of paper. Draw five feathers and cut them out. Make them a good size for your turkey. Use crayons to decorate the feathers. Glue the feathers together at the tips as shown at right.

6. Glue the tail onto the large end of the pine cone.

7. To make the place card, draw a small square or rectangle on a sheet of paper and cut it out. Write your name on the card. Put the card between two petals on the body so it will stand up.

33

Clay Menorah

What You Need

piece of flat, thin wood (about 6 inches [15 cm] wide and 14 inches [35 cm] long)

acrylic paints and paintbrushes

measuring cup

mixing bowl

spoon

flour

salt

cold water

Hanukkah candles

acrylic gloss medium, varnish, and brush *for teacher* (optional)

What You Do

1. For children who don't know what a menorah is, explain that it's a special candle holder used to celebrate Hanukkah, the eight-day Jewish festival of lights. The shammes candle is lit first and is then used to light the other candles, one for each day of the holiday. The number of candles lit is increased by one each successive night.

2. Paint the wood base and let it dry.

3. Make self-hardening clay by mixing together 1 cup (250 ml) flour and 1 cup (250 ml) salt, and gradually stirring in cold water until the mixture has a consistency good for modeling. Knead the clay. This recipe yields approximately the amount of clay needed for one menorah. If necessary, make more clay by mixing equal parts of flour and salt and stirring in cold water.

4. Shape the clay into a ball about 1 1/2 inches (4 cm) in diameter. Place the ball near the left edge of the wood base and center it widthwise. (More clay balls will run across the length of the base and be formed into candleholders.) Press the ball down slightly so the clay sticks to the base.

5. Insert a Hanukkah candle into the center of the ball, pressing it down to the bottom. Move the candle around in a circle, gently pressing it against the inner walls of the ball to make the opening just slightly larger than the candle. Remove the candle.

6. Make eight other clay holders in the same way, pressing them onto the wooden base, one next to the other. Raise the holder in the center for the shammes candle a little higher than the other holders by building up a small clay mound.

7. After the menorah has been modeled, allow the clay to dry thoroughly (about 5 days to a week).

8. Paint the menorah with acrylic paint and let it dry.

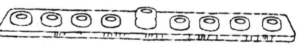

9. To protect the holder and base from candle drippings, the teacher or another adult may want to cover the menorah with a coat of acrylic gloss medium and varnish. Let the menorah dry overnight.

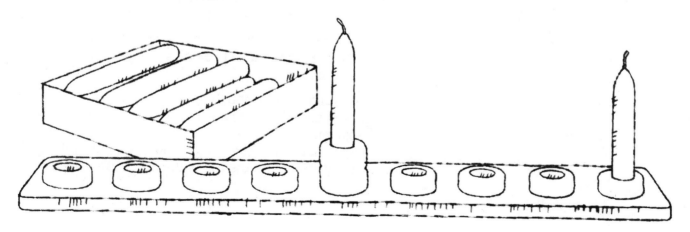

DECEMBER

Sponge Santas

and Other Spongy Shapes

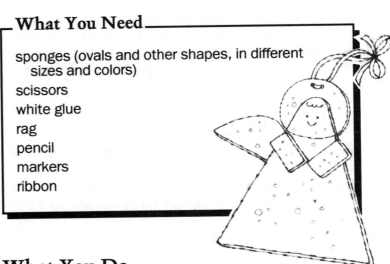

What You Need

sponges (ovals and other shapes, in different
   sizes and colors)

scissors

white glue

rag

pencil

markers

ribbon

What You Do

1. Ordinary kitchen sponges, cut and glued together, can be transformed into Santas, reindeer, elves, Christmas trees, angels, and so on. To make a Sponge Santa, begin with an oval sponge for the base. Use scissors to cut out rectangular arms and legs from another sponge and glue them onto the base (body). Press firmly so that the sponge pieces stick together. Remove excess glue by blotting with a rag.

2. Cut several other simple sponge shapes for Santa's hat, beard, and shoes and add them to his body. If needed, use a pencil to draw the shapes before cutting them out. Arrange sponge pieces and glue them onto the body.

3. Use markers to add some details, such as facial features and a belt buckle. Keep the marker lines simple.

4. Push a pencil all the way through the oval sponge near the top to make two holes, slightly apart from each other.

5. Thread a piece of ribbon through the holes from the front to the back. The Sponge Santa may be hung by adjusting the length of the ribbon and tying it at the top. Or the ribbon may be tied around a present, with the Sponge Santa on the top of the box or dangling from it.

6. Create other holiday "spongy" shapes to decorate the classroom.

Paste-String Ornaments

Paste-String Balls and Flat Paste-String Shapes

What You Need

small, round balloons

flour

water

bowl or other container (for paste)

spoon

thick string or yarn (different colors)

rag

pin

sheet of paper

tissue paper of different colors, scissors, white glue (optional)

Safety Note: Teacher or another adult should blow up balloons and then remove deflated balloons from ornaments.

What You Do
Paste-String Balls

1. Teacher or other adult should blow up the balloon and knot the end.

2. Mix together flour and water to form a very thick, creamy paste. Soak a length of string in the bowl of paste for a few minutes. Wipe off excess paste with a rag or by pulling it between two fingers.

3. Wind the string around the balloon in different directions to create open patterns and shapes. Wrap, loop, and crisscross to create free-form designs. Tell children to leave plenty of open areas or "windows" on the balloon. It shouldn't be completely covered with string.

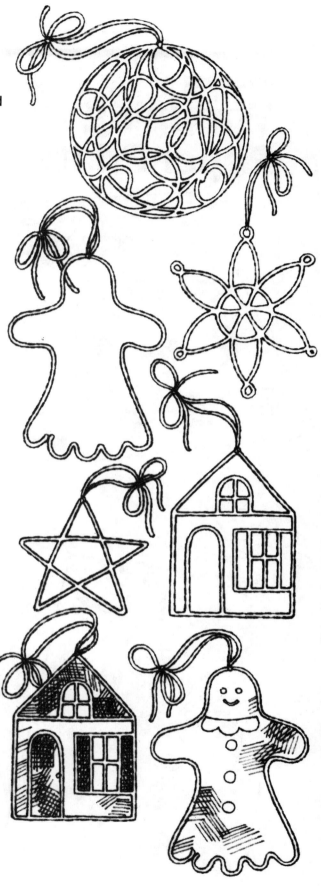

4. Hang the balloon up to dry overnight by tying a different piece of string (one not dipped in paste) onto the knotted end of the balloon.

5. When the paste-string dries, it will harden. Untie and remove the string used to hang the balloon. The teacher or another adult should pop the balloon with a pin and carefully remove the balloon (or balloon pieces) from inside the string ball. Slip the balloon out through an opening in the string design.

6. Tie a piece of string to the paste-string ball for hanging.

Flat Paste-String Shapes

1. Soak a length of string in the flour-water paste, remove, and wipe off excess.

2. Place the string on a piece of paper and arrange it into a special shape. Form the string into something realistic— a person, animal, star, house—or create an abstract design.

3. Allow the string to dry overnight.

4. When the string dries, it will stiffen. Gently remove the string shape from the paper. The paste-string ornament can be hung by string so that the entire open-weave shape is visible. Or it can be decorated further.

5. Decorate the ornament by pasting colorful tissue paper (traced and cut to fit space) to several of the open areas.

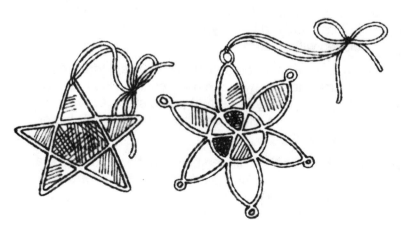

Wrapping Paper Prints

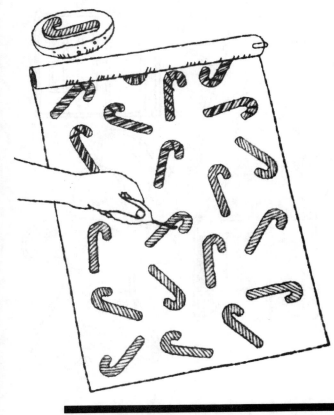

What You Need

roll of *uncoated* shelf paper (or brown wrapping paper)

scissors

empty cardboard paper-towel roll

paper clips (nonmetal, if available)

green leaves and/or vegetables (potato, carrot, cabbage)

string (for cabbage)

tempera and paintbrushes

flat trays or paper plates (for spreading paints)

scrap paper

newspaper

What You Do

1. Unroll about 4 (or more) feet (1.2 m) of uncoated shelf paper (or brown paper), cut, and distribute to each child.

2. Have children roll their sheets of paper onto empty paper-towel rolls, leaving about 2 feet (60 cm) of paper on their work space. Children will be printing on paper from their own "minirolls." They should secure the rolled paper with a paper clip.

3. Follow the basic steps for creating vegetable prints (pages 12–13) and leaf prints (page 16). Help children plan their wrapping paper designs by deciding what repeating shape or shapes they want to use.

4. Here are some suggestions for wrapping paper prints:

   ● Leaf patterns, printed in red and green (Christmas colors). Add red holly-type berries by printing small circles with a carrot.

   ● Draw a five-pointed star shape on the surface of a potato and cut away the background. Use this star stamp to print gold, red, or green stars. Create a six-pointed star for Hanukkah and print it using blue or silver paint.

5. When the area the children have printed on is dry, they can remove the paper clip and roll the paper onto the paper towel roll. Or they can unroll more plain paper and continue printing more wrapping paper.

New Year's Eve Noisemaker

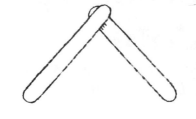

What You Need

wooden craft sticks
white glue
aluminum foil pie plates
pebbles, dry beans, or popcorn kernels
masking tape
ribbon (type that can be curled)
scissors
crayons
construction paper

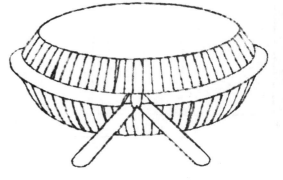

What You Do

1. Make a handle for the noisemaker by gluing two wooden craft sticks together to form a V-shape. Let the glue dry.

2. Put several handfuls of pebbles, dry beans, or popcorn kernels into an aluminum foil pie plate. Turn a second pie plate upside down and place it on top. Insert the V part of the wooden sticks in between the two plates. (The two *ends* of the *V* should be sticking out.)

3. Tape the foil plates tightly together on either side of the two sticks and between them. Then use masking tape to seal all around the edges of the plates so that the contents do not shake out later.

4. Cut ribbons into pieces about 12 inches (30 cm) long. Tape them onto the rim at desired intervals around the plates. Teacher or another adult should pull the ribbons across the cutting edge of a pair of scissors to make them curl. This will create the effect of New Year's streamers.

5. Use crayons to color the masking tape. Then decorate the rest of the noisemaker. Here are some suggestions: Make drawings of New Year's hats on construction paper, cut them out, and tape them to the noisemaker with rolled-up pieces of masking tape. Or punch holes near the tops of little cutouts of New Year's hats and tie them to the dangling ribbons.

6. Children will enjoy shaking their noisemakers on New Year's Eve!

Pop-Up Greeting Card

Pop up with your own special holiday greetings!

What You Need

construction paper
pencil
scissors
crayons or markers

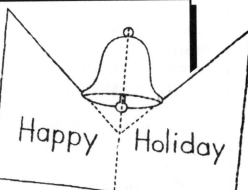

What You Do

1. Fold the paper in half.

2. Bring the top left-hand corner down to the opposite side to form a triangle. (You will have a rectangle left at the bottom.) Press along the fold of the triangle. Then fold the paper back the other way along the fold to crease the triangle. Fold it forward again, pressing along the fold.

3. Open up the paper.

4. Fold the top of each triangle inward to make this shape.

5. Open up the paper again. Decide what holiday design you want to pop up. Here are some ideas: a bell, a Christmas tree, a star, a special gift, a candle. Draw your holiday pop-up shape in the space shown.

6. Cut from the corners down to the outline of the pop-up shape and around the top of it.

7. Use crayons or markers to decorate your pop-up card. And don't forget to add a special holiday message!

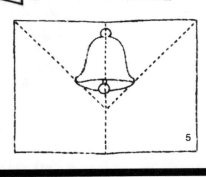

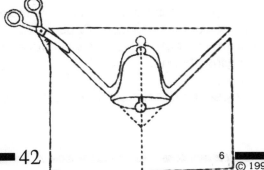

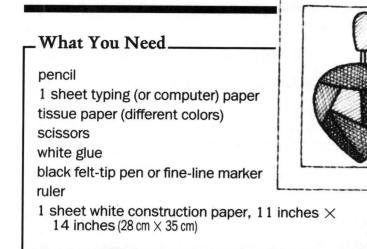

What You Need

pencil
1 sheet typing (or computer) paper
tissue paper (different colors)
scissors
white glue
black felt-tip pen or fine-line marker
ruler
1 sheet white construction paper, 11 inches ×
   14 inches (28 cm × 35 cm)

Stained-Glass Toy Shop Windows

Have you ever seen a stained-glass window? Stained glass is colored glass that is cut into shapes and joined together to make pictures in such things as windows, lamps, and boxes. Turn your classroom windows into toy shop windows with stained glass!

What You Do

1. Draw the outline of your favorite toy on a sheet of typing (or computer) paper.

2. Divide the design into sections by drawing pencil lines. This will make the picture look as if it were created with pieces of glass.

3. Place one color of tissue paper over your design. Trace the shape of one section onto the tissue paper. Cut out the tissue paper shape. Glue it onto the matching shape on the typing paper.

4. Choose your colors and trace each section. Cut and glue until you have filled all sections of the design.

5. Use a black pen or marker to draw lines separating the sections.

6. Make a "window frame" using white construction paper. Measure and draw a rectangle slightly larger than the typing paper. Leave about 1 1/2 inches (4 cm) on all sides. Cut out the center.

7. Place the frame on top of the toy design. Then glue the typing paper onto the frame.

8. Hang your toy design in a classroom window together with your classmates' designs to create a toy shop window. Watch the light shine through the "stained glass"!

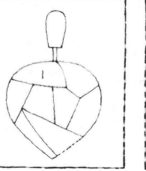

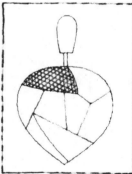

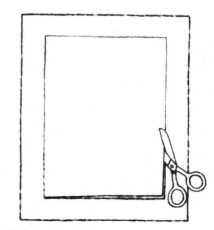

Soap-Snow Mural and Soap-Clay Snowballs

What You Need

large sheet of brown paper (size of mural)
pencil
tempera and paintbrushes
soap flakes and soap powder
water
measuring cup
2 large mixing bowls
eggbeater
large spoon
string or ribbons

Soap-Clay Recipe:

1/2 cup (125 ml) water
2 cups (500 ml) soap flakes or soap
   powder

Beat water and soap in a large bowl until mixture begins to harden. Add more soap until mixture has the consistency of dough. Stir with spoon if the mixture is too thick to beat. (*Note:* Children must dip hands in cold water prior to using mixture so that it doesn't stick to their hands.)

Children should knot a piece of string or ribbon and place it in the center as they shape soap clay into snowballs. Hang snowballs by string or ribbon after the soap clay has dried.

What You Do

1. Plan a winter mural as a group activity. Tell children it will be a snowy outdoor scene, and help them make a sketch to show how the mural will look. Explain that all parts of the mural should be integrated into a coordinated scene.

2. Divide the class into groups, each to paint a specific section of the mural (children playing in the snow, building snow figures, sledding, ice-skating, making snow angels, and so on). Children should use *thick* tempera. Before the paint dries, they should sprinkle the area with a light coat of soap powder. The powder will stick to the surface and will give the effect of light snow. Shake off excess powder.

3. Thicker "soap snow" can be added to the mural. Children might use this soap snow for a snowman or a snow-covered hill. It will stick wherever it is placed. To make snow from soap, pour some soap flakes into a mixing bowl, slowly add some water, and beat continuously with an eggbeater.

4. While some groups of children are painting, others may wish to make hanging soap-clay snowballs. (The soap-clay snowballs will begin to crumble in about a week.)

Pattern Rollers

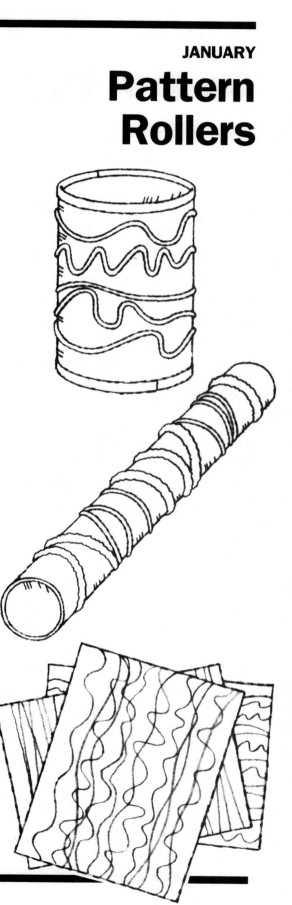

rollers: empty cardboard tubes (from paper towels and toilet paper); empty cardboard frozen-juice cans; empty tin cans (with both ends removed and wrappings left on)

glue

string or yarn

rag

tempera and paintbrushes

trays or paper plates (for spreading paint)

white drawing paper

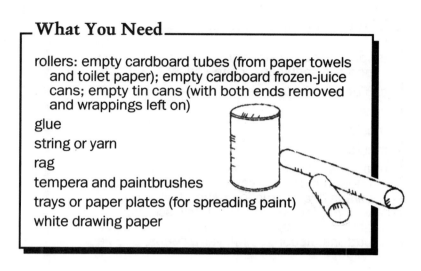

Safety Note: Cover the cut edges of tin cans with masking tape.

What You Do

1. Squeeze or brush glue onto the outside of the can or tube roller. Leave the area near both open ends unglued.

2. Wind string or yarn around the roller. Open areas should be left as the string is wound. Some areas can be wide apart, others close together. Wipe off excess glue with a rag. Allow the glue on the roller to dry.

3. Spread one color of tempera in a tray or on a paper plate. If children are using a tin can, have them put one hand on either end of the roller and roll it in the paint to cover the string. Add more paint with a paintbrush, if necessary. If children are using a cardboard roller, several fingers (middle, index, ring fingers) can be inserted inside the roller, with the thumb and pinky on the outside.

4. Roll the can or tube with paint-covered string or yarn onto white drawing paper to make repeating patterns. Rollers can be rolled in different directions to overlap existing patterns, creating new patterns.

5. For variations, experiment by rolling a tube or can with a second color of paint and different string arrangement onto the paper. (Wait until the first color has dried.) Or try using a roller with string glued to one part and yarn to the other.

Tin Can Zoo

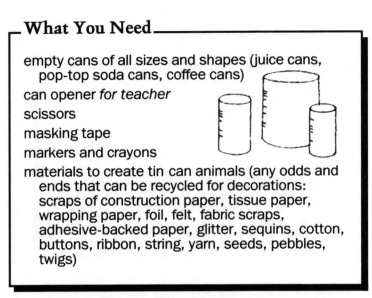

What You Need

empty cans of all sizes and shapes (juice cans,
  pop-top soda cans, coffee cans)
can opener *for teacher*
scissors
masking tape
markers and crayons
materials to create tin can animals (any odds and
  ends that can be recycled for decorations:
  scraps of construction paper, tissue paper,
  wrapping paper, foil, felt, fabric scraps,
  adhesive-backed paper, glitter, sequins, cotton,
  buttons, ribbon, string, yarn, seeds, pebbles,
  twigs)

Safety Note: Teacher should use the can opener to punch any holes needed as children create their animals. Tape over any jagged or sharp edges as soon as holes are punched.

What You Do

1. Tell children that tin cans can be recycled into animals of all types. Together children can create a "tin can zoo."

2. Prepare cans by peeling away or soaking off paper wrappings. Clean the inside thoroughly with soap and water. Remove any glue from the outer surface. Dry the cans.

3. Encourage children to use their imaginations to create a variety of zoo animals. Have them experiment by holding cans upright or on their sides and arranging them with other cans and different materials until they can visualize the animal they want to create.

4. Fasten cans together with masking tape for tall giraffes or camels with humps. Connect cans with string or ribbon to make long, slithery snakes, or lions with tails. Add felt or cut paper for facial features, elephant ears and trunks, or penguin flippers. Stick twigs into holes in the can top to make deer antlers. Use yarn for a horse's mane or zebra's stripes. Tape together paper straws or wooden craft sticks (decorated with sequins and glitter) for a peacock's tail fan. Try coverings of felt and cotton for a furry panda. A big paint can makes for a great tin can hippopotamus!

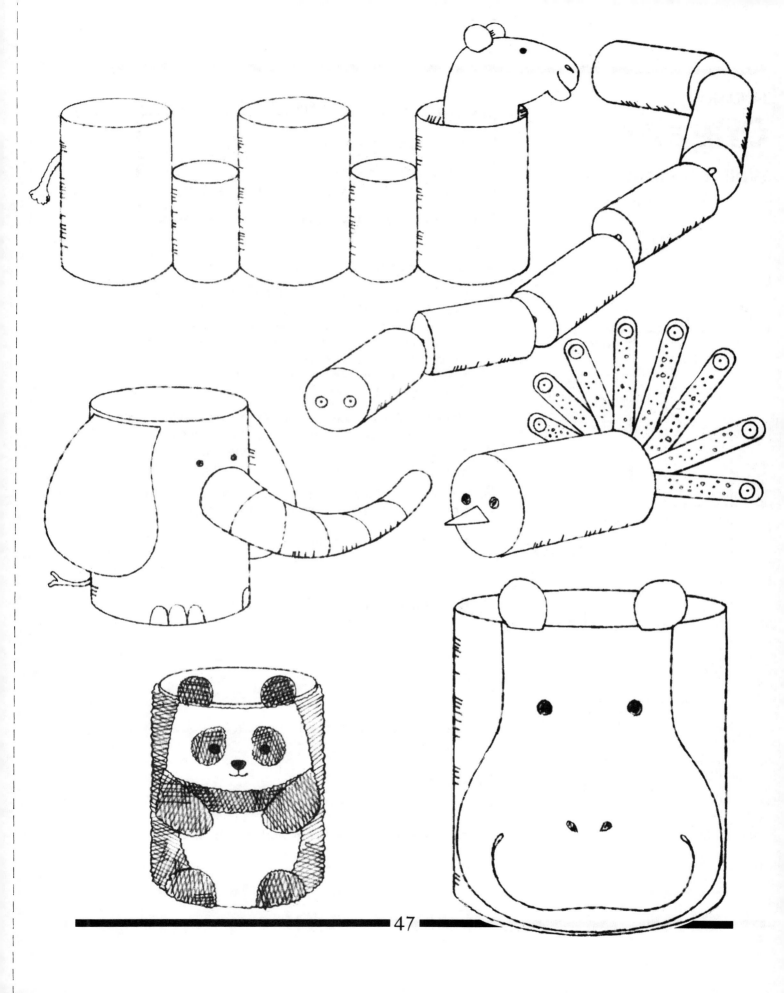

Origami

Wallet and Boat

rectangle

square

a.

What You Need

origami paper (or wrapping paper, newspaper, or other thin paper that is flexible, folds well, and holds a good crease)

scissors (to cut rectangular paper into a square)

What You Do

1. Tell children that origami is the Japanese art of paper folding. Objects like birds, boats, and boxes are made from a single sheet of paper without pasting or cutting. The word *origami* comes from two Japanese words: *oru* means "to fold" and *kami* means "paper." When the words were combined, the pronunciation was changed to make the word *origami*.

2. Work on a flat surface and make the folds. Origami folds should be creased carefully by pressing a finger or fingernail along the fold each time one is made. If paper tears or crumples, take a new sheet and start again.

3. Begin with a square piece of paper. Here is how to make a paper square from a rectangular piece of paper:

   a. Fold corner end to side.

   b. Cut along edge.

   c. Unfold.

The folding of the wallet and the boat are both traditional Japanese origami projects.

Wallet

Make an origami wallet by following these steps:

   a. Fold square paper in half and crease. Unfold.

b. Fold the sides up to the horizontal center line. Turn the paper over.

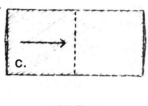

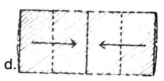

c. Fold the paper in half to create a vertical crease. Unfold.

d. Fold the sides to the vertical center.

e. Fold the paper in half.

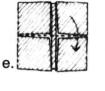

f. Finished origami wallet has two pockets.

Children can slip "lucky pennies" into the pockets of their origami wallets. The wallets might also come in handy for math lessons that involve money.

Boat

Make a boat by following these steps:

a. Fold square paper in half and crease. Unfold.

b. Fold the sides up to the horizontal center line.

c. Fold each corner down to the horizontal center line.

d. Fold the corner of each rectangle (labeled "d") down to the center line.

e. Fold triangular points (labeled "e") down to center line.

The folded paper should look like this:

f. Open center and turn inside out for finished boat.

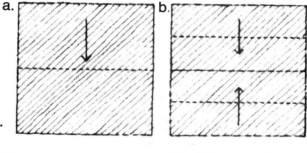

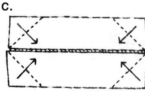

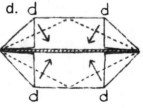

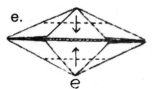

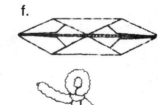

Children can make pipe cleaner figures to put in their boats.

Animal Sock Puppets

Socks make wonderful puppets. You can save old socks and use them to create all kinds of animal puppets.

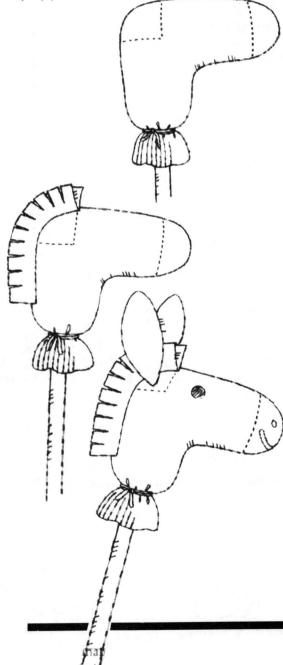

What You Need

1 large sock
old nylon stockings (or other material for stuffing)
a long, strong stick (The cardboard roller from a wire hanger works well.)
string
scissors
scraps of felt
2 buttons (for eyes)
glue

What You Do

1. Stuff the sock with old nylon stockings or other stuffing. Pack the stuffing in tightly, so that the sock is stiff. Fill the sock to about 2 inches (5 cm) from the opening.

2. Push a stick up into the sock through the stuffing to the heel.

3. To attach the stick to the sock, wrap the string around the end of the sock at least four times. Tie it tightly.

4. Decorate the sock, making any animal you like.

5. For example, here's how to make a donkey puppet. A donkey's mane is usually shorter than a horse's mane and stands straight up. Use two pieces of felt about 2 inches (5 cm) wide and 7 inches (17 cm) long. Cut 1-inch (2.5-cm) slits along one side of each piece of felt.

6. Glue the unslit sides of the pieces of felt along the center of the sock, starting from the top of the heel and down toward the ankle. Position the two pieces of felt close enough together that they lean on each other and create a mane that stands up.

7. Make the face. A donkey's ears are larger than a horse's ears. Cut out two felt ears and glue them on each side of the head. Glue on buttons for eyes. Cut out a felt mouth and two small circles for nostrils. Glue them into place on the sock.

8. Use the stick to make your animal sock puppet move.

50

Paper Snowflake Mobile

What You Need

white construction paper (squares and circles; use a cup or bowl to trace a circle the size of the snowflake you want)

scissors

wire hanger

thread

A mobile is a sculpture that moves. Its parts are made from paper, wood, or other material. The movable parts hang down from wire or string. They're arranged so that they balance and can float freely in space. Make a paper snowflake mobile to decorate your classroom!

What You Do

1. To make a snowflake, fold a white paper square or circle in half.

2. Fold the paper in half again. Then fold it in half once more.

3. Make interesting cutouts along the edges, as shown. Try notches, slits, and squiggles.

4. Open the paper to see your snowflake design. Fold and cut other snowflakes. In nature, no two snowflakes are alike. Try a variety of designs.

5. To make the mobile, ask an adult to help you twist open a wire hanger. Bend it as shown, or in a similar way.

6. Tie a length of thread through one of the openings near the outer edge of a snowflake. Add different lengths of thread to the other snowflakes. Hang all but one snowflake on the mobile.

7. Find out where the *balance point* of your mobile is. It depends on the weight and arrangement of the snowflakes. Rest the wire crossbar on your fingertip to find the spot where the mobile does not tilt.

8. Tie a piece of long thread onto the bar at that balance point. The thread will be used for hanging the mobile. Tie the last snowflake at that spot. Hang your mobile and watch the snowflakes float in the air.

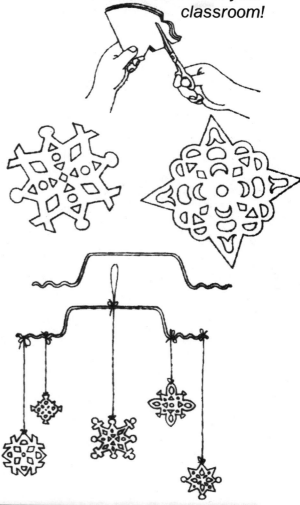

Rolled Newspaper Log Cabin

What You Need

newspaper (cut into sheets about the size of typing paper)
pencil
white glue
scissors
cardboard
construction paper, 9 inch × 12 inch (22 cm × 30 cm)
masking tape
markers (for roof, optional)

What You Do

1. Children can honor Lincoln's birthday by building a log cabin with rolled newspapers. The shape of rolled paper is a natural for logs—and a good way to recycle old newspapers.

2. To make a log, roll a sheet of newspaper (cut as described above) tightly around a pencil. Apply glue to the end of the newspaper and press it down along the entire length to make sure it sticks. Slide out the pencil. If necessary, push the pencil out with the point of another pencil. Roll and glue a batch of paper logs (at least 24) to use for building the cabin. Children can work in pairs, with one child gluing and the other building.

3. The logs will be glued together to construct the cabin. Place two newspaper logs on a sheet of cardboard, in a parallel position about 6 inches (15 cm) apart. Place two more logs in a perpendicular position over the first two logs, so that a "square" of four logs is formed. When they're positioned, glue the top two logs onto the bottom ones. Let the glue dry.

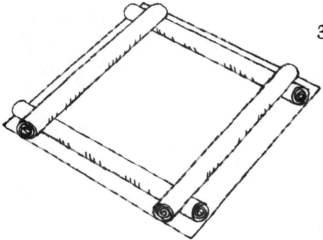

4. While the glue is drying, prepare five or six more squares of four logs each. Allow the glue to dry for each square.

5. Build up the model by adding each of these square groups to the cabin. Let the glue dry thoroughly before another layer is added.

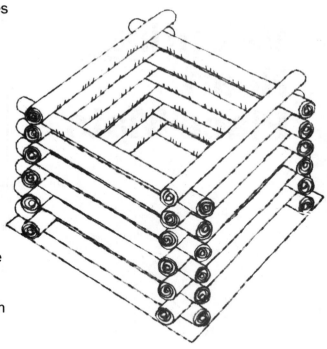

6. Make a roof with "shingles." Bend a sheet of construction paper in half and then fold under 1/2 inch (1 1/4 cm) along the bottom edges. Cut a small chimney hole in the side of the roof. Add shingles in one of the following ways:

  a. Roll and glue more sheets of newspaper and cut the rolls into pieces about 1 1/2 inches (4 cm) long. Glue the smaller rolled logs onto the construction paper without covering the chimney hole. Leave a 1/2-inch (1 1/4-cm) border up from the folded edges.

  b. Cut and glue flat newspaper pieces onto the construction paper to look like shingles.

  c. Use markers to draw shingles on the construction paper.

7. Add the roof to the top of the log base, fitting the folded part inside the two top logs of the cabin walls. Insert a small rolled log into the hole for the chimney and tape the bottom underneath the roof.

Children can create rolled newspaper models of many other buildings—from bridges to windmills!

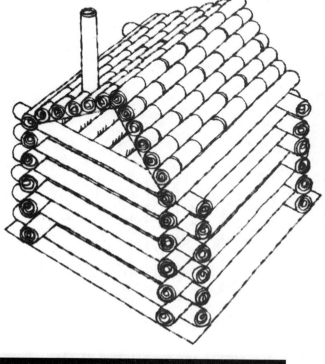

FEBRUARY

Valentine Heart Place Mats

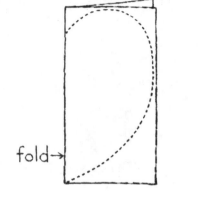

fold→

What You Need

red felt (12 inches × 12 inches [30 cm × 30 cm])
white or pink felt (12 inches × 12 inches
   [30 cm × 30 cm])
ruler
pencil
scissors
white glue

What You Do

1. Tell children that this Valentine's Day they can "weave" their way into someone's heart by making a heart-shaped place mat. Use a piece of red felt for the heart. Fold the felt in half and draw half a heart on it.

2. Keeping the felt folded, cut along the outline, making sure to cut through both layers of felt.

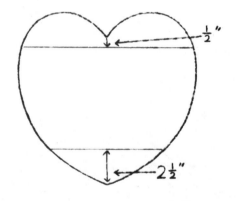

½"

2½"

3. Open the heart and measure about 1/2 inch (1 1/4 cm) down from the top. Using a pencil draw a line across the heart. Measure another 2 1/2 inches (6 cm) from the bottom and draw another line across the heart.

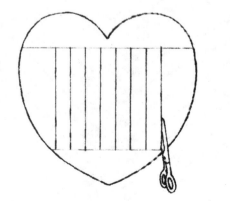

4. Measure and draw vertical lines about 1 inch (2 1/2 cm) apart across the width of the heart. Cut slits along each line.

5. In preparation for weaving the heart, measure 1-inch (2 1/2-cm) strips on the white (or pink) felt. Make sure there are at least seven strips measured, then cut them out. (Save the leftover felt for another project.)

6. To weave the white (or pink) strips into the red heart, start at the top of the heart. Push the white felt under the first slit, over the second slit, under the third, and so on. Continue to weave under and over until the white strip is woven into all of the slits.

7. Weave the next white strip directly under the first, but this time begin by weaving *over* the first slit, under the second, over the third, and so on. Continue weaving until the entire heart is filled in.

8. Trim any white (or pink) strip ends that extend beyond the edges of the red heart. Use white glue to secure the woven strips on both ends of the heart.

Have children bring their heart place mats home and give them to a lucky valentine!

Sponge Print Valentine's Cards

What You Need

construction paper (different colors)
sponges
scissors
tray or shallow dish (for spreading paint)
tempera

What You Do

1. Children can print their own Valentine's cards with sponges. Have them fold a sheet of construction paper in half for each card they want to make.

2. Use scissors to cut sponges into heart shapes. Children may work with one heart sponge or a number of heart sponges in different sizes.

3. Pour some paint into a tray or shallow dish and spread it out. (Keep in mind the color of the paper when selecting the paint color.) Lightly dip one side of the sponge into the paint, placing it flat against the tray so that the entire surface is covered.

4. To print, press the painted side of the sponge against the front cover of the card. Then carefully lift the sponge straight up.

5. Make a design of hearts on each card. Create a repeating heart design by pressing the sponge on the card many times, using one color of paint or several. Combine prints from sponge hearts of various sizes. Open the card and print on the back cover as well as the front. Or create wraparound prints from front cover to back.

6. Tell children to add "hearty" messages to their sponge print Valentine's cards!

During the year, children can cut sponges into other shapes, and design and print cards for every occasion.

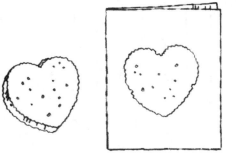

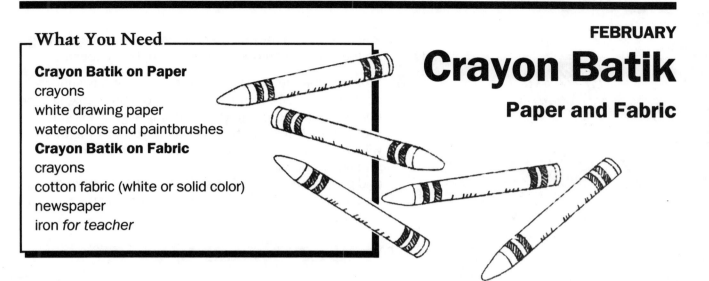

Crayon Batik

Paper and Fabric

What You Need

Crayon Batik on Paper
crayons
white drawing paper
watercolors and paintbrushes

Crayon Batik on Fabric
crayons
cotton fabric (white or solid color)
newspaper
iron *for teacher*

Safety Note: Make sure children do not go near hot iron.

What You Do

Encourage children to create crayon batik pictures (on either paper or fabric) that carry environmental messages. After discussion, suggest that each child draw a picture to show one way he or she can help the environment. Drawings might depict a child planting a tree or flowers, hanging a homemade bird feeder, picking up litter, recycling cans, using a pump-spray product (*not* aerosol), bringing a cloth bag to carry groceries home from the supermarket, and so on.

Crayon Batik on Paper

1. Use crayons to color the environmental pictures on white drawing paper. Leave areas of background uncolored so that there is ''white space'' in the picture.

2. Paint over the entire sheet of drawing paper with watercolors. The paint resists the crayon wax markings, adhering only to those spaces left uncolored.

Crayon Batik on Fabric

1. Use crayons to draw the environmental pictures on fabric. Press down to make solid areas of color. If needed, put a weight (such as a book or heavy stone) on each end of the fabric to hold it in place while drawing. Or hold down the fabric with one hand.

2. Place a sheet of newspaper on top of the fabric drawing so that the crayon markings are completely covered.

3. Teacher or another adult can then iron the newspaper-covered fabric. To remove the wax from the batik, set the iron to *dry* (not steam). Use a setting slightly lower than that suggested for cotton. As the crayon wax melts, it will be absorbed by the newspaper. The pigment will remain on the fabric. Remove the first newspaper sheet and put another sheet in its place to absorb more of the wax. Continue replacing the newspaper until the wax no longer comes off the fabric.

What You Need

self-hardening clay
thin piece of wire (optional)
crayons
tempera and paintbrushes

Pinched-Clay Crayon Pot

You can make a pot to hold crayons, using your fingers as tools. You'll be pinching the clay—squeezing and shaping it with your fingers—to make a "pinch" pot.

What You Do

1. Before you shape the pot, take all the air bubbles out of the clay by *kneading* or *wedging*. Choose either of these ways:
   a. *Kneading.* Take a large handful of clay. Put it on a desk or table. Knead by turning the clay over and over and pressing down into the center with the palms of your hands.
   b. *Wedging.* Take a large handful of clay. Put it on a desk or table. Cut it in half with a piece of wire. Throw one half of the clay onto the table. Then throw the second half on top of it. Knead the clay, slice it in half, and throw it again. Keep doing this until you don't see any air bubbles when you cut the clay. Then it's ready.

2. To shape the pot, roll a handful of clay into a ball. Hold the ball in the palm of one hand. Press the thumb of your other hand into the center of the ball.

3. Pinch the clay together with your thumb and index finger while turning the ball around and around. Do this until the ball looks like a pot. Try to make the walls of the pot even in thickness. If the clay gets too dry, wet your fingers to smooth and soften it. Damp fingers will help get out rough spots and cracks.

4. Shape the pot so that it's a good size for crayons. You can hold a crayon next to the pot to measure. Make sure there's room inside for many crayons and that the pot isn't too tall. The tops of the crayons should stick out.

5. Let your Pinched-Clay Crayon Pot dry thoroughly. Turn it on its side after a few days so that the air dries the bottom. Drying time takes about a week.

6. When the pot dries, use tempera to decorate it.

7. Put crayons in the pot. Or use your pot for other things. To store paper clips, simply change the name to "Pinched-Clay Clip Pot"!

59

Fingerprint Postcards

You can print with just about anything—even your fingers! Try making postcards stamped with your own fingerprint designs.

What You Need

your fingers
tempera
small flat tray or paper plates (for paint)
stiff 3½" × 5" (9 cm × 13 cm) card
felt-tip pen or fine-line marker
pencil
ruler

What You Do

1. Pour a little tempera into a flat tray or onto a paper plate.

2. Press one of your fingertips into the paint. Then press your finger onto one side of the card. You've made your first fingerprint!

3. Let the paint dry. Then use a felt-tip pen or fine-line marker to add a few details. Turn the print into anything you'd like. Here are some ideas:

   a. Do repeating prints to make a caterpillar. Cover your card with a zooful of animals.

   b. Combine prints of different fingers. Your thumbprint can be the center of a flower. Make pinkie prints for the petals. Use repeating prints from your index finger to make a turtle's shell. Add a thumbprint for the turtle's head and pinkie prints for its feet.

   c. Create a whole fingerprint family with prints from each of your fingers.

4. Use only one color paint for all the prints on your card. Or make prints in many different colors.

5. When you finish your postcard design, let the paint dry. Turn the postcard over. Use a pencil and ruler to draw a line down the middle. Write your message on the left side and put the mailing address on the right. Add a postage stamp. Mail your fingerprint postcard to a friend.

6. If you have a lot to write, use your fingers to print stationery and matching envelopes!

60

Decorative Eggs

Batik, Patchwork, and Curly Ribbon Eggs

What You Need

hard-boiled eggs/large raw eggs
needle *for teacher*
bowl
scissors
white glue
newspaper (for drying eggs)

Batik Eggs
white crayon
food coloring, vinegar, measuring spoon, measuring cup

Patchwork Eggs
scraps of different fabrics

Curly Ribbon Eggs
ribbons (different colors, curling kind)

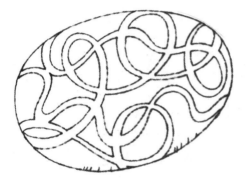

What You Do

For Batik Eggs:
Use hard-boiled eggs.

For Patchwork Eggs and Curly Ribbon Eggs:

1. Tell children they will use raw eggs with the insides blown out of their shells.

2. Working over a bowl, teacher or another adult should use a needle to puncture a small hole at one end of a raw egg. Make a slightly larger hole at the other end.

3. Child should blow gently into the smaller hole so that the egg comes out of the hole at the other end. (*Safety Note:* To avoid ingestion of raw egg, do not allow children to put their mouths to the eggs. They need only to have their mouths near enough to the hole in one end of an egg to blow into it. Have children wash their hands with soap and water after blowing eggs.) Rinse out the egg with water and set it aside to dry. Preparation of the eggs may be done at home, and the empty eggshells brought to school. Children can prepare as many eggs as they'd like to decorate.

Batik Eggs

1. Remind children that batik is a method of making designs on a surface by putting wax on the parts they

don't want dyed. They can create batik eggs using dyes and a crayon.

2. Draw a design on an egg with a white crayon. Try repeating a special pattern. Or make free curving, swirling lines. Remind children that the parts where they draw with their crayon will remain white when they dye the egg.

3. Follow this recipe for making the dye. To 3/4 cup (180 ml) boiling water, add 2 teaspoons (10 ml) vinegar and about 15 drops of food coloring for the desired shade. Stir. *Safety Note:* After teacher or other adult boils the water and pours it into a teacup, closely supervise the children as they add the vinegar and food coloring.

4. Roll the egg in the cup of dye. When it's the desired shade, remove the egg from the dye with a spoon. Place the batik egg on a sheet of newspaper to dry. The area designed with the crayon will remain white and the background will be colored with dye. The design will stand out against the background.

Patchwork Eggs

1. Tell children that patchwork is a design made up of different sizes, shapes, and colors of material that have been put together. Have them cut scraps of different fabrics into square and rectangular shapes about the size of postage stamps.

2. Dab some glue onto an area of the egg. Stick one piece of fabric onto the glued area. Add glue to a part of the egg next to the first area and place a piece of fabric onto it, overlapping the first piece of fabric.

3. Keep adding glue and scraps of fabric, placing them in different directions, with different degrees of overlap. Cover the entire surface of the egg, including the holes at each end. When the egg is covered, smooth down all of the fabric to make certain all of the patches stick to the egg. Place the patchwork egg on a sheet of newspaper to dry.

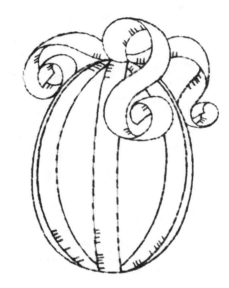

Curly Ribbon Eggs

1. For each egg, cut three or four pieces of ribbon—each about 5 inches (13 cm) long. Teacher or another adult should pull the ribbon pieces around the cutting edge of a scissors to make them curl. Leave about 1 1/2 inches (4 cm) of the ribbon uncurled. Cut other ribbons into pieces about 1 1/2 inches (4 cm) long. (The length needed for each egg will vary.)

2. Apply glue to the flat part of a piece of the curled ribbon. Stick it to the egg lengthwise with the curled top at the tip of the egg. Add the other curled ribbon pieces to other sections of the egg so that the curls meet at the top.

3. Glue the shorter pieces of ribbon onto the egg, creating a vertical design. Not all of the egg surface needs to be covered with ribbon. White eggshell spaces between the lengths of ribbon can be an effective part of the design.

Suggest that children "hatch" some egg ideas of their own!

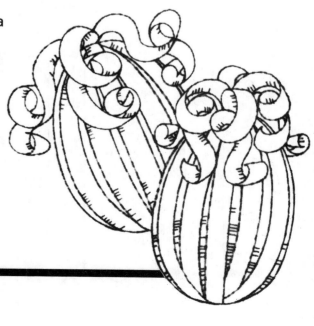

Tube Eggheads

What You Need

empty blown eggshells (Prepare in same way as for Batik, Patchwork, and Curly Ribbon Eggs, page 61.)

tempera and paintbrushes

empty cardboard tubes (from paper towels or toilet paper)

scissors

construction paper (different colors)

white glue or masking tape

ball of cotton

What You Do

1. Tell children that they can turn eggs into heads of bunnies, chicks, and other animals associated with spring.

2. Hold the egg in a vertical position. Use tempera to paint on features that give the eggheads personalities of their own. Make them happy, sad, surprised, or just plain funny-looking. Paint one part of the egg at a time, and allow the painted area to dry before children continue.

3. Use empty cardboard tubes from paper towels or toilet paper as egghead stands. The finished egg will sit in the opening of the tube.

4. The tube itself can become part of the animal's body. Design the body tubes before putting the heads on. Consider the length of the tube. Create a funny bunny with a long body (paper towel roll) in relationship to the tiny size of its egghead, or use more realistic proportions.

5. Add details to the tube. Glue a cotton ball tail to a bunny body tube. Construction paper bunny feet can stick out from the bottom. Yellow paper wings and orange feet can be glued or taped onto the tube body of a chick.

6. When both the head and body are designed, rest the egg in the tube. The tube eggheads will make heads turn!

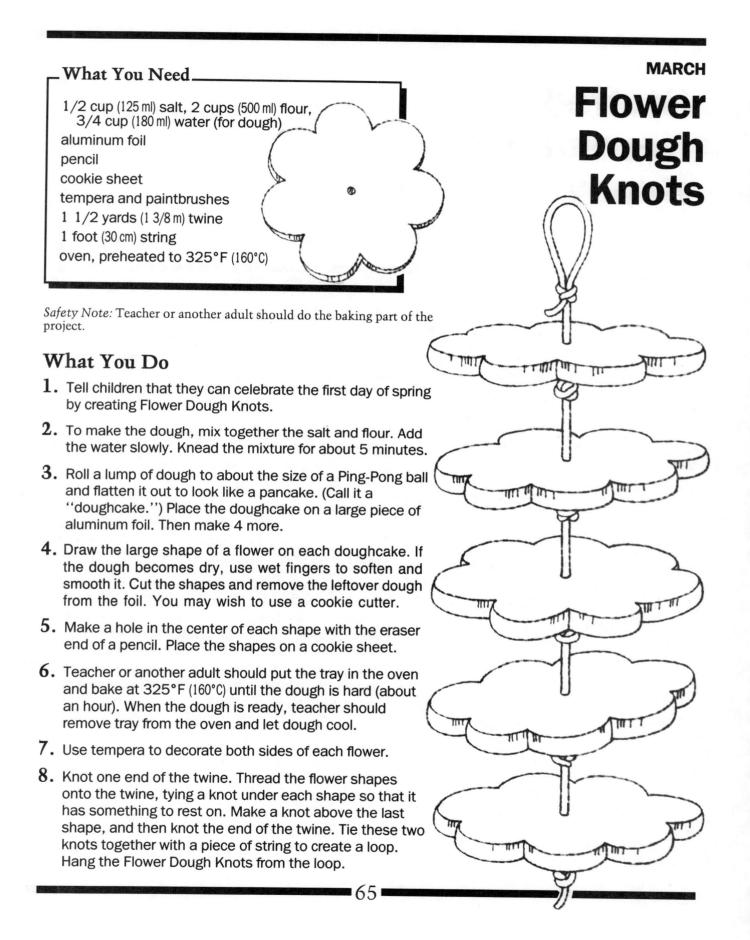

Flower Dough Knots

What You Need

1/2 cup (125 ml) salt, 2 cups (500 ml) flour, 3/4 cup (180 ml) water (for dough)

aluminum foil

pencil

cookie sheet

tempera and paintbrushes

1 1/2 yards (1 3/8 m) twine

1 foot (30 cm) string

oven, preheated to 325°F (160°C)

Safety Note: Teacher or another adult should do the baking part of the project.

What You Do

1. Tell children that they can celebrate the first day of spring by creating Flower Dough Knots.

2. To make the dough, mix together the salt and flour. Add the water slowly. Knead the mixture for about 5 minutes.

3. Roll a lump of dough to about the size of a Ping-Pong ball and flatten it out to look like a pancake. (Call it a "doughcake.") Place the doughcake on a large piece of aluminum foil. Then make 4 more.

4. Draw the large shape of a flower on each doughcake. If the dough becomes dry, use wet fingers to soften and smooth it. Cut the shapes and remove the leftover dough from the foil. You may wish to use a cookie cutter.

5. Make a hole in the center of each shape with the eraser end of a pencil. Place the shapes on a cookie sheet.

6. Teacher or another adult should put the tray in the oven and bake at 325°F (160°C) until the dough is hard (about an hour). When the dough is ready, teacher should remove tray from the oven and let dough cool.

7. Use tempera to decorate both sides of each flower.

8. Knot one end of the twine. Thread the flower shapes onto the twine, tying a knot under each shape so that it has something to rest on. Make a knot above the last shape, and then knot the end of the twine. Tie these two knots together with a piece of string to create a loop. Hang the Flower Dough Knots from the loop.

Stuffed Newspaper Bunny

What You Need

newspaper
pencil
scissors
hole punch
paper clips
thin string
tempera (or acrylic paints) and paintbrushes
round looseleaf-paper reinforcements

What You Do

1. Tell children they can make a big three-dimensional bunny or other shape out of newspaper stuffed with newspaper. Each child should decide on a shape— anything from a bunny or spring chick to a bird, butterfly, or beetle.

2. Spread out two sheets of newspaper, one on top of the other. Draw the outline of the bunny or other shape on the top sheet, covering as much surface as possible to make it big.

3. Cut along the outline through both sheets, keeping them together so that the cut shapes are an *exact* match. Crush the trimmed-off newspaper into a ball and put it aside to use later for stuffing.

4. Keeping the newspapers lined up, punch holes all around the outer edge, about 1/4 inch (1/2 cm) in from the edge. Space holes about 1/2 inch (1 cm) apart. Caution children not to punch holes too close to the edge. They should hold the newspapers together while working, using paper clips in several spots, if needed. If papers slip, children can insert a pencil into the holes to line the two sheets up again.

5. Cut a long piece of string. Thread one end through a paper hole. Attach a paper clip to the other end, allowing about 5 inches (13 cm) of string to dangle. Sew or weave the threaded end in and out of the holes until a little more than half of the shape has been sewn.

6. Insert small wads of newspaper inside the shape. Keep stuffing until the entire shape is full. Then continue sewing the rest of the figure. Make sure to hold the edges of the two newspaper sheets together, lining up the holes.

7. When back at the starting point, remove the paper clip and tie the two ends of string together. Knot the string several times and cut off the end. *Note:* If children missed any holes or any areas are spaced too far apart, simply staple together the edges of the two newspaper sheets in those spots.

8. Paint the shape with tempera or acrylic paints, making it colorful and fun. Allow paint to dry. Additional material may be added to the shape, such as a ball of cotton for a bunny tail.

9. Stick a round looseleaf-paper reinforcement on the front and back of the two adjacent holes at the top of the head. Insert a length of string through the reinforced holes and hang the stuffed newspaper shape.

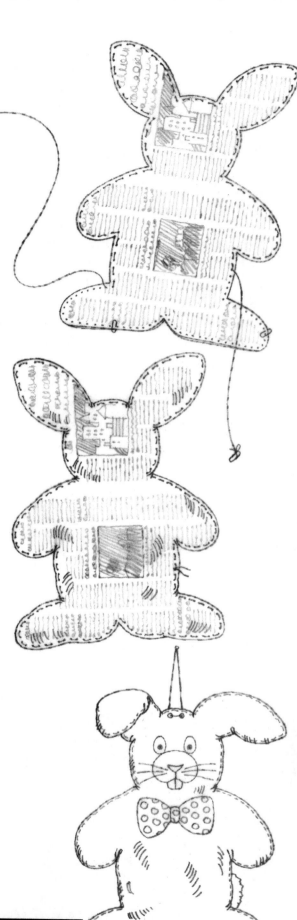

Shamrock Leis

In Hawaii, you might be greeted with an aloha and a Hawaiian lei. Aloha means "love" in Hawaiian and is used to mean hello and good-bye. Leis are wreaths, or necklaces, made of fresh flowers. A shamrock is a kind of clover with three leaflets. It's the emblem of Ireland. Greet someone this St. Patrick's Day with a Shamrock lei!

What You Need

2 packages of paper napkins (Napkins should be 2 different colors. Try to get 2 shades of green or green and another color.)
1 sheet of cardboard
pencil
scissors
2 yards (1 7/8 m) of strong cotton thread
needle

What You Do

1. Draw the shape of a shamrock on the sheet of cardboard. A shamrock looks like this:

Since you will trace the shamrock four times on one folded napkin, make it an appropriate size.

2. Cut out the cardboard pattern. Leaving the napkin folded, trace the shape on the top left-hand corner. Trace around this pattern three more times on the napkin.

3. Hold several napkins together and cut out the patterns. Continue tracing and cutting patterns.

4. Thread heavy cotton thread through a needle and knot the two ends together so the thread is doubled. (If you need help, ask your teacher to do the threading and knotting.) String the napkin shamrocks onto the thread. Use about 1 inch (2 1/2 cm) of one color and then change to the other. Switch colors in this way along the entire length of the thread.

5. When the thread is full, cut it right below the needle and knot the two ends together.

Windsock

March is known as "the windy month." Try making a paper bag windsock to catch some of the breeze!

What You Need

ruler

pencil

large paper grocery bag—bottom should measure about 17 inches x 12 inches (43 cm x 30 cm)

tempera and paintbrushes

wire, 20 inches (50 cm) long

5 pieces of thick string—4 pieces 12 inches (30 cm) each, 1 piece 6 feet (1 7/8 m)

masking tape

What You Do

1. Draw a 4-inch (10-cm) circle on the bottom of a large paper bag and cut it out.

2. Place the bag flat. Use tempera to paint designs on all sides. Let each side dry between paintings.

3. Bend a piece of wire into a circle 6 inches (15 cm) in diameter. Tape together the two ends of the wire.

4. Tie the four pieces of 12-inch (30-cm) string around the rim of the wire. Space them evenly. Wrap a piece of masking tape around the wire over each tied part to keep the string from slipping.

5. Knot the four pieces of string together at the ends. Tie the 6-foot (1 7/8-m) piece of string to the knotted ends. This long string will be used to hang your windsock.

6. Open the bag and put the wire circle into the bottom. Center it over the hole with the strings hanging outside. Tape the wire to the bottom of the bag in a few spots to hold it in place.

7. Hang your windsock from the long piece of string. Have an adult help you tie it to a pole or tree branch. When the March wind blows through the windsock, the bag will fly in the breeze. Each time you look at your windsock, you will see how strong the wind is and the direction it is blowing.

69

Spring Flowers

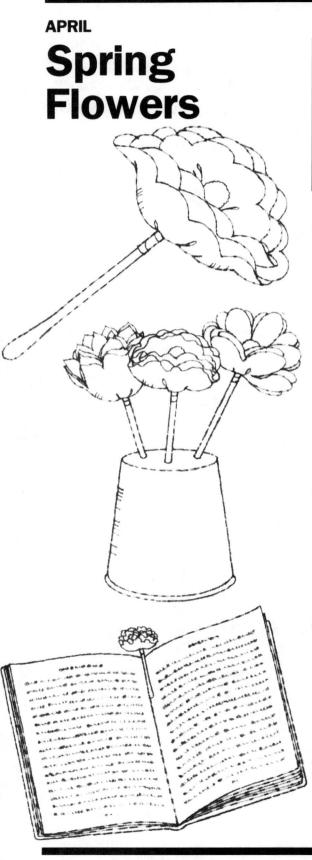

cotton swabs
tempera and paintbrushes
crepe paper (different colors)
pencil
scissors
paper cups (for flower holder; optional)

What You Do

1. Dip the tip of a cotton swab into tempera. This will be the colorful center dot of the flower. Allow the cotton tip to dry. Paint the "stem" of the swab green and put it aside to dry.

2. Lightly draw a flower shape (about 3 inches [7 1/2 cm] in diameter) on a piece of crepe paper. Put two other pieces of crepe paper underneath and cut out all three pieces.

3. Hold the identical shapes together and push a pencil point through the center to make a small hole. Poke the painted tip of the cotton swab up into the hole, creating both the center of the flower and the stem.

4. Bunch up each of the petals and pinch with your fingers to create the desired shape. Then pinch the flower together at the base.

5. Cut a thin strip of crepe paper, brush it with glue, and twist it around the cotton swab and the base of the flower. This will hold the completed flower in place.

6. Cut shapes for a bouquet of flowers: daisies, lilies, tulips, and so on. If desired, create a crepe paper flower arrangement in a paper cup. Invert the cup and have the teacher or another adult make small scissor slits in the bottom. Insert the end of the swab stem so that it is wedged in the slit with the flower sticking up out of the base.

7. Individual flowers may be used as bookmarks. Put the stem between pages, with the petals peeking out at the top of the book.

Fruit and Vegetable Rubbings

Class Cookbook

What You Need

fruits and vegetables (orange, pineapple, grapefruit, celery, carrot, cabbage, cucumber, corn on the cob, onion, potato with little knobs or shoots)

knife *for teacher*

tissue paper (different colors)

crayons (with paper wrappings removed)

construction paper

glue

hole punch

ribbon

What You Do

1. Rubbings can be made from the outer surface of many fruits and vegetables and the inside textures of some. Not all fruits and vegetables make good rubbings. Very soft fruits will not work, and those that have smooth surfaces will not yield a textured effect. All the fruits and vegetables above can be used to make good rubbings.

2. Cut the fruit or vegetable into slices or in half. Make the resulting surface flat. To help seal in juices, allow cut fruits and vegetables to dry overnight.

3. Cut away any protruding hard parts (like a stem). Put a piece of tissue paper over the surface of a fruit or vegetable and rub the paper with the side of a crayon (wrapping removed). Because tissue paper is thin and can tear, rub a small area at a time with strokes in one direction.

4. Try rubbing over the kernels of an ear of corn, the outside of a pineapple, or a wedge from a head of cabbage. Experiment with grapefruit, oranges, celery, cucumbers, onions, and carrots.

5. Make a class cookbook of fruit and vegetable rubbings and recipes. Suggest that each child contribute a recipe to go with a particular rubbing. Each section of the cookbook might focus on a particular fruit or vegetable.

6. Glue the edges of the vegetable rubbings and the recipes to sheets of construction paper. Punch holes in the sides of the construction paper pages and thread ribbon through the holes to bind the class cookbook.

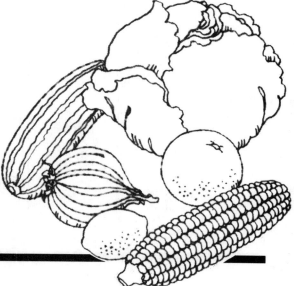

Birdhouses

Milk Carton and Milk Jug

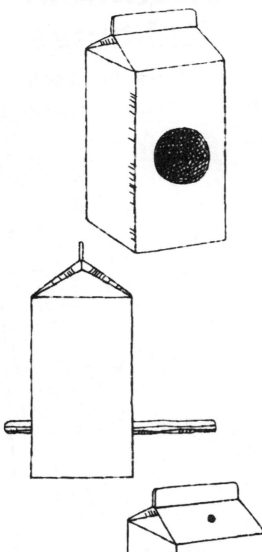

What You Need

empty half-gallon (2-liter) cardboard milk (or juice) container or gallon (4-liter) plastic milk jug

pencil

scissors

sturdy twig, about 1 foot (30 cm) long (for perch)

wire, about 2 1/2 feet (76 cm) per house; easy to bend, strong enough for hanging birdhouse

shipping tape

acrylic paints and paintbrushes (for plastic jug)

What You Do

Tell children they can recycle milk cartons and jugs into homes for birds. The houses will be placed for birds to rest and nest. Wash and dry the cardboard carton or plastic jug thoroughly. The preparation of the birdhouse will vary slightly depending on which type of container is used. Both options are given.

Milk Carton Birdhouse

1. Use a pencil to poke a hole in the side of the carton, about halfway up. Use scissors to enlarge the hole. (Teacher or another adult may need to help cut the hole, depending on the age and ability of the child.) Make the hole an appropriate size for the type of bird that might come calling. The hole is the door to the birdhouse.

2. Poke another pencil hole slightly below the entrance for a twig. Insert a sturdy twig through the hole, pushing it to the opposite side of the carton. Mark the spot on the outside and poke another hole at that point. Push the twig through the second hole and position it so that equal lengths of twig stick out at the front and back of the birdhouse. This twig will serve as a perch for the bird.

3. To hang the birdhouse, make two more pencil holes in the top roof-shaped part of the carton as shown.

4. Thread the wire through the top holes. If necessary, open the spout of the container and reach inside to guide the wire from one hole to the other. Both ends of the wire should now hang outside the carton. Seal the spout closed with shipping tape. Teacher or another adult should hang the birdhouse by twisting the two ends of wire around the branch of a tree. Make sure the birdhouse is securely fastened.

Milk Jug Birdhouse

1. An adult should cut out a door hole about halfway down the jug. Since plastic edges are jagged and sharp, tape all around the hole with shipping tape. With scissors, poke a small hole in the front and back of the jug for the bird perch and tape around the edges.

2. To decorate the birdhouse, children can paint the plastic bottle with acrylic paints, creating their own special designs.

3. Insert a twig through the two holes for the perch.

4. With scissors, teacher or other adult can poke two holes through the top of the jug and thread wire through them. Twist the two wire ends together for hanging.

Children will enjoy watching the birds move into their milk carton and milk jug birdhouses.

Foil Sculpture

head→

←body

leg piece→

←foil sheet

basic body shape

FOILED AGAIN!

aluminum foil
ruler
scissors
scraps of felt
white glue
3 feet (90 cm) of yellow ribbon (for each foil lion, cut into 2-inch [5-cm] pieces)

What You Do

1. Since foil is extremely pliable, it can be twisted, pinched, rolled, and so on. It's a perfect material for sculpting. Children might enjoy making this foil lion. Then they can create a zooful of other aluminum animals.

2. Children can make a basic shape, which with bending can be turned into any animal they want. Measure and cut 3 feet (90 cm) of foil. Crush it to form the head and the body. Crush an 18-inch (45-cm) piece of foil (leg piece) and bend it in half over the first piece, about 3/4 of the way from the head end. Fold the body portion over the leg piece to hold it in place.

3. Crush another 18-inch (45-cm) sheet of foil to form the arms. Hold the arms in place by molding a sheet of foil over the head and down the back.

4. Continue adding crushed sheets of foil to form various parts of the body. Pinch the foil lightly until a definite shape is formed.

5. To make a lion, bend the basic shape into a sitting position so that the arms become the lion's front legs. Make sure that the front legs are touching the desktop or tabletop. Build up the body with several layers of foil. Don't forget to make a tail.

6. Create the lion's face by gluing felt scraps onto the head. Make eyes and a nose and a mouth. Glue foil ears onto the sides of the lion's head. Make a mane by looping together the ends of each 2-inch (5-cm) ribbon piece. Glue the loops onto the head.

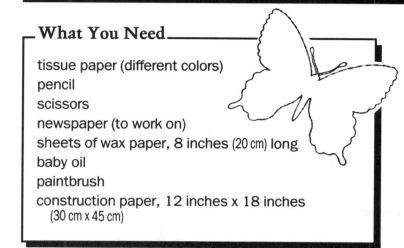

What You Need

tissue paper (different colors)
pencil
scissors
newspaper (to work on)
sheets of wax paper, 8 inches (20 cm) long
baby oil
paintbrush
construction paper, 12 inches x 18 inches
   (30 cm x 45 cm)

Oiled Wax Paper Pictures

Fliers and Crawlers

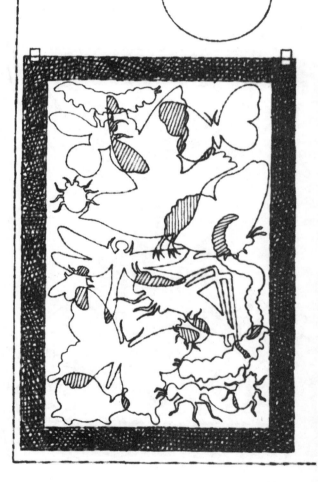

What You Do

1. Draw and cut out tissue paper shapes about 3 inches (7 1/2 cm) to 4 inches (10 cm) in diameter. Create shapes of spring "fliers and crawlers" such as snails, worms, ants, ladybugs, butterflies, birds, and so on.

2. Spread out sheets of newspaper to work on. Squirt an S-shape of baby oil onto a sheet of wax paper and smooth it out over the entire surface with a brush. Apply the oil thickly so that the tissue paper can soak it up.

3. Press and smooth the tissue paper shapes onto the wax paper, overlapping the pieces until they cover the entire sheet of wax paper. New colors will be created where the pieces overlap. If any of the pieces haven't soaked up the oil, brush a little more oil over the tissue paper.

4. Put another sheet of wax paper on top. Rub over both sheets. Press firmly so that the top wax paper sheet sticks onto the tissue paper. Pick up both sheets, with the tissue paper sealed in between the sheets.

5. Press the sheets between three or four sheets of newspaper and allow the picture to dry thoroughly. Change the newspaper a few times during the drying process. Drying can take about a week.

6. Make a frame by folding a 12 inch x 18 inch (30 cm x 45 cm) sheet of construction paper in half. Cut a "window" out of the paper, leaving a 1-inch (2 1/2-cm) border all around. Insert the wax paper picture inside the frame and staple the papers together.

7. Hang the Oiled Wax Paper Pictures on a window. On a sunny day brilliant light will fly and crawl all over the spring shapes.

APRIL
Wildflower Plate Hanging

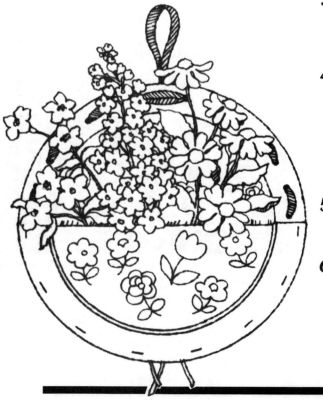

What You Need

wildflowers, rubber band, wire hanger
large white paper plates (uncoated)
scissors
crayons or markers
ruler
hole punch
ribbon or yarn

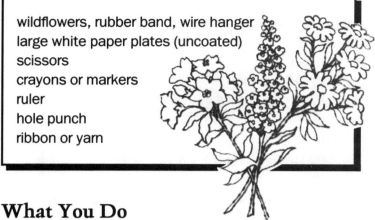

What You Do

1. Dry a bunch of wildflowers by attaching them to a wire hanger with a rubber band and hanging them upside down. Drying takes one to two weeks (see page 14).

2. Cut a large white uncoated paper plate in half. Have an uncut paper plate on hand, too. Use crayons or markers to design the front, top half of a whole plate and the back of a half-plate. Since the half-plate will become the outside bottom of the whole plate (a "pocket" for the wildflowers), tell children to consider the "whole" picture.

3. To make the holder, put the half-plate over the whole plate (fronts together) and line up the edges to make a pocket. Staple the plates together at the edges, with staples about 2 inches (5 cm) apart from one another.

4. Punch holes all around the rim of the top half of the whole plate. Weave a long piece of ribbon or yarn through all of the holes, knotting it on both ends behind the plate. Thread another piece of ribbon or yarn through the two top center holes (over the other ribbon). Tie the ends together into a loop that will later be used for hanging the plate.

5. Arrange the dried wildflowers inside the paper-plate pocket (the half-plate), with stems sticking through the open areas between the staples.

6. Hang the plates around the classroom as spring decorations. Some extra wildflower plates may be made as a class effort and hung on the door. Children can tell classroom visitors (parent volunteers, special speakers, etc.) to "pick a flower" from the pockets to take home with them when they leave.

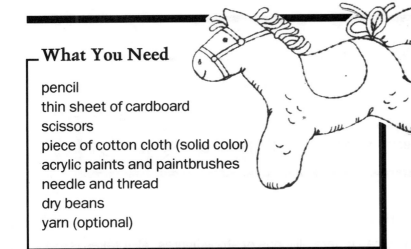

What You Need

pencil
thin sheet of cardboard
scissors
piece of cotton cloth (solid color)
acrylic paints and paintbrushes
needle and thread
dry beans
yarn (optional)

Beanbag Animals

Play catch this spring with a beanbag animal.

What You Do

1. Draw the side view of an animal on a piece of cardboard. Make the shape about the size that you'd like your beanbag to be. Cut out the shape.

2. Fold a piece of cloth in half. The folded cloth should be bigger than your animal. Cut the cloth in half along the fold. Then put one piece on top of the other.

3. Trace around the cardboard pattern onto the top cloth. Keeping the cloth pieces together, cut out the animal shape. You will have two pieces that are the same.

4. Use acrylics to paint one side of your animal on each piece of cloth. Keep in mind that the pieces will be matched up and sewn together; paint only the two sides that will face out. Paint the animal's face, legs, and tail. Add special details such as a trunk, mane, horns, spots, or stripes. Let the paint dry completely.

5. Put the pieces of cloth together so that the painted sides face each other. Sew around the edges, leaving an opening about 2 1/2 inches (6 cm) wide. Knot and cut the thread.

6. Turn the animal bag right-side out. Fill about 3/4 of the bag with dry beans.

7. Sew the rest of the bag. Turn the edges under as you sew.

8. You can tie a piece of yarn tightly around the cloth to make your animal's tail or trunk stick out. You might sew on pieces of yarn for a lion's or horse's mane.

Straw Figures

You've sipped lemonade with straws, and blown bubbles with them. But have you ever tried building robots, alien creatures, or friendly monsters with straws?

What You Need

paper drinking straws (large box)
scissors
stapler
heavy thread or string (for hanging)

What You Do

1. You can create all kinds of straw figures. All it takes is your imagination . . . and plenty of straws. Try to picture what your straw figure will look like. Draw a picture first, if it helps you. You'll be using a stapler to join the paper straws together.

2. Begin by making the head. Staple two straws together, or bend one straw and staple it to itself. Add more straws. Twist, loop, and bend. Crease and cut. Shape and staple straws to make the head into a circle, square, triangle, or rectangle.

3. Here are some ideas: Give an alien creature some straw antennas. Wind and staple straws into small shapes for a robot's eyes. Make a gigantic smiling straw mouth for a friendly monster. Add lots of straw teeth.

4. Let your shape "grow" by adding more straws for the rest of the body. Make your figure as big and fun as you like.

5. Figure out how to make your straw figure stand and balance on its feet. Or hang it by looping a piece of string or thread through an opening in the top.

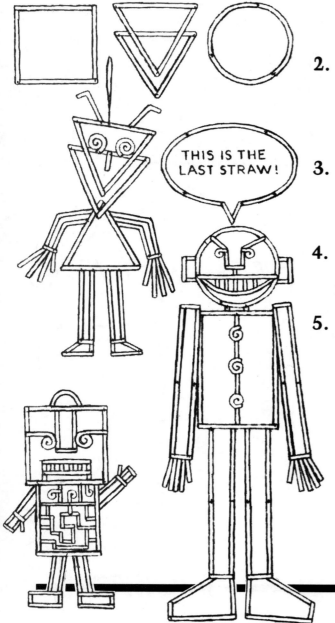

THIS IS THE LAST STRAW!

Magazine Bead Necklaces

What You Need

old magazines (colorful pages)
scissors
pencil
white glue
thin yarn

What You Do

1. Tell children that they can recycle magazine pages into beautiful beads and string them onto necklaces.

2. Tear out colorful pages from old magazines. Cut different-sized triangles from the pages. The base of each triangle should be fairly narrow. (Tall, thin triangles work well.) Children will need to try different sizes to see what works for their necklaces. Mixing triangle sizes creates a nice effect.

3. Remind children of the rolled newspaper log cabin they made (page 52). The principle for rolling beads is the same. Roll the base of the triangle around a pencil until you reach the point of the triangle. Dab some glue onto the point and press until the glue sticks. Remove the bead from the pencil. If desired, use scissors to snip the edges straight across. Or leave more pointy ends on the beads.

4. Roll and glue many other magazine beads until there are enough for a necklace.

5. Cut a piece of yarn a little longer than the desired length of the necklace. String the beads and knot the ends together. Magazine Bead Necklaces are fun to wear and make great gifts.

Pasta Bracelets and Necklaces

What You Need

Tube-shaped pasta (or any pasta shapes with a hole through the middle, such as wagon wheels; various sizes and shapes)

tempera and paintbrushes, or food coloring and water

container or dish

newspaper (to work on)

scissors

narrow elastic, thin yarn, or ribbon (for stringing)

large-eyed needle

Safety Note: Teacher or another adult should carefully supervise children as they string pasta with needles.

What You Do

1. Tell children they can color the pasta shapes in one of two ways:
   a. Paint pasta with a thick coat of tempera. Allow one side to dry before painting the other.
   b. Put 4 or 5 drops of food coloring into a dish of water, adding more drops to get the deepness of color desired. Soak the pasta in the food coloring. Remove pasta and let it dry on a sheet of newspaper before stringing.

2. Cut a piece of narrow elastic, thin yarn, or ribbon slightly longer than the desired length for the bracelet and necklace.

3. Discuss some design considerations with the children before they do the stringing. They should think about variations in color, size, and shape of the pasta. If only one shape of pasta is used for the entire piece of jewelry, the use of color plays a particularly important role in the design. Children might want to use lots of bright alternating colors, or one color for both end sections and a contrasting color for the middle section.

One color can be used throughout when a bracelet is strung with pasta of different sizes and shapes. Or a different color can be used for each different shape. Each variation creates a different effect.

4. If children are using small pasta, thread a needle with thin elastic and insert it through the openings. Pasta with wide openings can be strung without a needle onto elastic, yarn, or ribbon. After stringing, knot the ends together. Pasta jewelry makes a great gift for Mother's Day and is also fun for the children to wear.

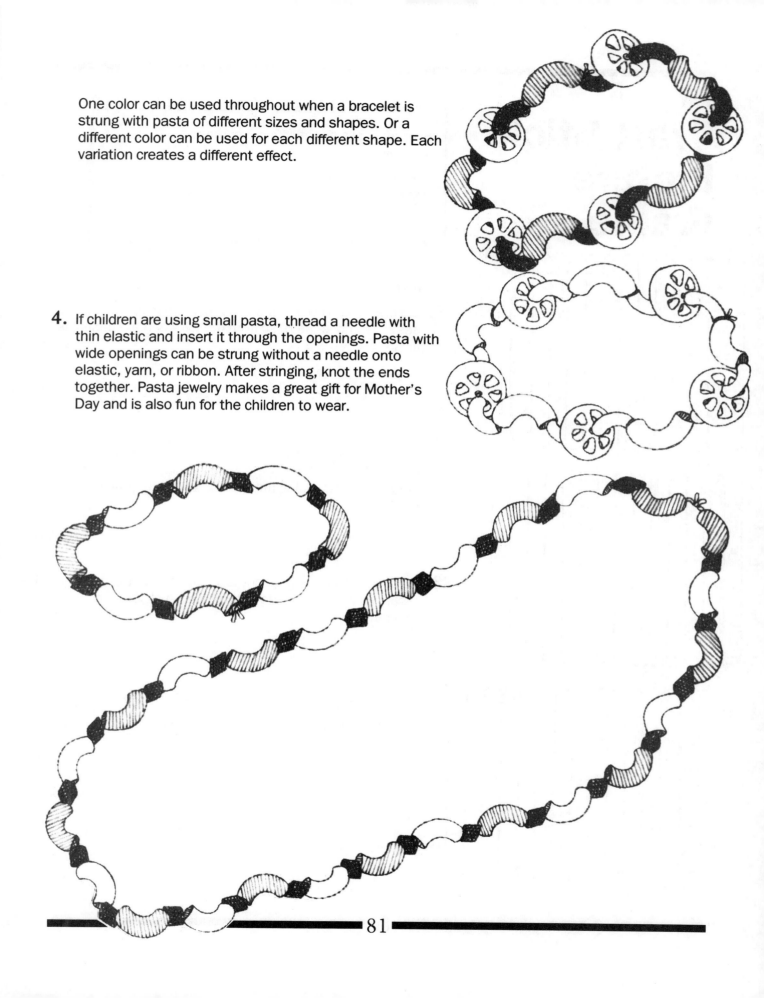

Craft Stick Picture Frame

What You Need

50 craft sticks (for each picture frame)

white glue

aluminum foil (to work on)

a special photograph (of child with Mom if intended as a gift for Mother's Day)

What You Do

1. Children should work on a sheet of aluminum foil. It's easy to remove the base from the foil when the project is finished.

2. Use 14 sticks for the base. Line them up side by side and glue them together by putting glue along the edge of one stick and attaching the second stick to the glued edge. Continue gluing until all 14 sticks are attached.

3. To build the frame, glue one stick directly on top of the first stick on the left side of the base (stick *A* in the diagram).

4. Put a drop of glue on the *A* stick, about an inch from the bottom. Glue stick *B* to stick *A* as shown.

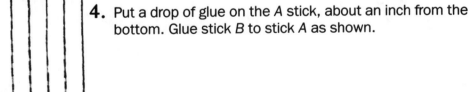

5. Following the diagram, glue *C* onto *B*, *D* onto *C*, *E* onto *D*, and *F* onto *E* and *A*. Continue adding sticks to this frame in the same manner as for *A* through *F*.

6. Children will have built up six levels around the frame when they've used all the remaining sticks. Allow the glue about half an hour to dry.

7. Glue a photograph onto the base. If children are planning to give Mom the picture frame for Mother's Day, they might choose a photo of themselves with Mom. Or they can use a photo of themselves, their entire family, their pet, and so on.

8. The Craft Stick Picture Frame can be hung from the opening in the top, propped up on a shelf for display, or laid flat on a desk or dresser.

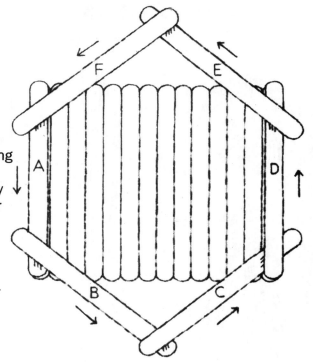

Yarn Dolls

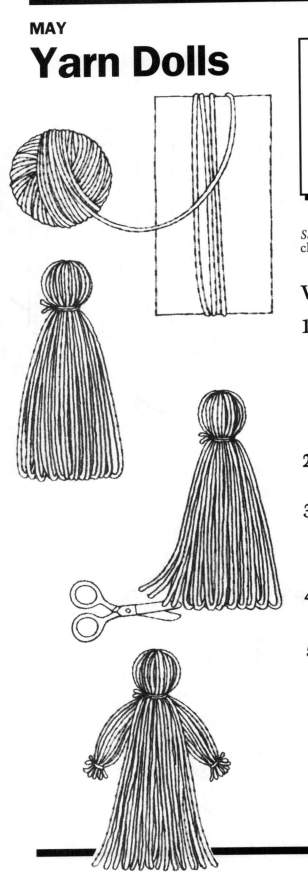

What You Need

sheet of heavy cardboard, cut to 5 inches ×
   10 inches (12.5 cm × 25 cm) or 9 inches ×
   12 inches (23 cm × 30 cm)

thick acrylic yarn

scissors

scraps of felt, needle and thread (optional, for
   facial features)

Safety Note: Teacher or another adult should carefully supervise
children who are sewing.

What You Do

1. Wrap yarn lengthwise around a sheet of cardboard,
   about 50 times. The doll will grow fuller, the more yarn is
   wrapped. (If using a 9 inch × 12 inch (23 cm × 30 cm) piece
   of cardboard, wrap the yarn around either the length or
   the width, depending on the desired height of the doll.)
   Don't wrap the yarn too tightly.

2. Carefully slip the yarn off the cardboard.

3. To make the head, tie another piece of yarn tightly
   around the lengths of yarn (a little way down from
   one end).

4. Cut open the loops at the bottom of the doll.

5. To make arms and hands, lift up some strands of yarn on
   each side and tie them tightly at the "wrist" with string.

6. Tightly tie a piece of yarn about halfway down the body for the waist.

7. The finished doll has a long, loose skirt. Or it can be given pants. Split the yarn into two sections below the waist. Tie a piece of string near the bottom of each section to create pants legs. Trim off any longer hanging pieces to even the doll at the bottom.

8. If desired, facial features may be cut out of felt and sewed onto the doll.

Paper Cup Totem Poles

Many Native American tribes, especially those of the Northwest, made totem poles. Wooden carvings of birds and animals on a totem pole showed the figures who were legendary in a certain family. Here's an unusual way to construct a totem pole.

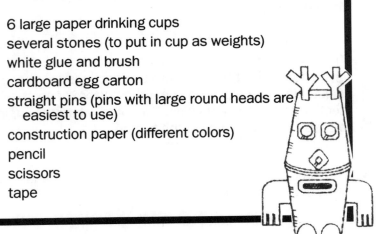

What You Need

6 large paper drinking cups

several stones (to put in cup as weights)

white glue and brush

cardboard egg carton

straight pins (pins with large round heads are easiest to use)

construction paper (different colors)

pencil

scissors

tape

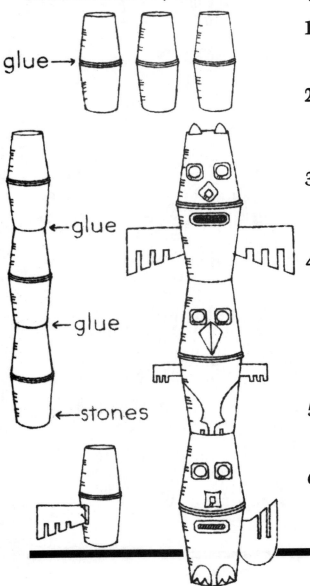

glue →

← glue

← glue

← stones

What You Do

1. Put several heavy stones in a cup. Glue the top rim of another cup onto that cup. Then glue the top rims of two other pairs of empty cups together. Let the glue dry.

2. The pair of cups with the stones will be the base. This base will keep the "pole" from toppling over. Stack the other pairs of cups on top of the base and glue the connecting bottoms. Let the glue dry completely.

3. Use your imagination to come up with all sorts of figures (birds, animals, people) for your totem pole. Here's an idea: Use an egg carton to decorate. Cut three egg cups and one pointed divider from the carton.

4. Use two of the egg cups for eyes. Put them in place with the hollow part facing in, so that the cups stick out. Push pins at angles through the edges of the egg cups into the drinking cup. Use the pointed egg carton divider for the nose. Pin it in place. Add an egg cup with the hollow part facing out for the mouth. Shape it by pressing the sides of the egg cup together, then pin the shape in place.

5. Make a pair of wings with construction paper. Fasten them by bending back the edge of the paper and sticking pins into the cup. (You can add a little tape, if needed.)

6. Decorate the rest of your totem pole. Use colorful construction paper and other *light* material. Make beaks, eyes, noses, mouths, wings, horns, arms, and tails that stick out from the totem pole.

What You Need

fresh flowers
very heavy book
wax paper or paper towels
construction paper
pencil, ruler, scissors
white glue
piece of scrap paper
clear plastic wrap and plastic tape

Pressed Flower Bookmarks

Flatten fresh flowers in a book and then use them to mark the place.

What You Do

1. Spread out fresh flowers side by side (*not* overlapping) between two sheets of waxed paper or paper towels. Place them between two pages at the end of a very heavy book. Put the book down flat on a desk, table, or shelf. The book will "press" the flowers, making them flat when they dry. To prevent mildew, check the flowers every four days or so. Each time you check, put them between fresh pieces of wax paper or toweling and insert them between different pages of the book. Drying time will take one to two weeks.

2. When the flowers have dried, you can put them onto bookmarks. Cut bookmarks from a sheet of construction paper. Some suggested sizes are: 8 inches × 2 1/2 inches (20 cm × 6 cm), 7 inches × 2 1/2 inches (18 cm × 6 cm), and 6 inches × 2 inches (15 cm × 5 cm).

3. To get an idea of what your bookmark will look like, arrange a flower (or several flowers) on one paper bookmark. The dried flowers are very delicate, so handle them carefully.

4. When you like your sample, pick up the flowers and dab some drops of glue onto the bookmark. Put the flowers on top of the glue. Put a piece of scrap paper over the flowers and smooth very gently with your hand. Take off the scrap paper and let the glue dry.

5. Cover your Pressed Flower Bookmark with clear plastic wrap and tape it on the back. Any "bookworm" is sure to be imPRESSed with these flowers!

Seashell Memo Clips and Pads

What You Need

typing or computer paper

scissors

masking tape

crayons (with paper wrappings removed)

small seashells and pebbles (at least one seashell should have a textured surface, as a scallop shell does)

wooden clothespins (clamp-type, not forked)

acrylic paints and paintbrushes

newspaper (to work on and for drying)

white glue

What You Do

1. Children can make memo clips with matching memo pads for Father's Day. They can also keep the clips on their desks for school memos. To make the memo pad, fold and cut a sheet of typing or computer paper into eight pieces.

2. Tape the underside of a small shell with a textured surface to a desk or tabletop. Place one of the memo sheets over the shell and rub with the side of an unwrapped crayon. The rubbing should be made near one of the corners, to allow writing space for the memo. Make shell rubbings on all eight pieces of paper.

3. To make the memo clip, paint a wooden clamp-type clothespin with acrylics. Paint one side first, let it dry on a sheet of newspaper, and then paint the other half.

4. Glue small seashells and little pebbles in an interesting arrangement onto the top surface of the clothespin. Leave about one third of the clothespin—the handle end—without shells or pebbles. Decorations at that end could fall off when fingers open and close the clothespin.

5. Clip the Seashell Memo Pad sheets with the Seashell Memo Clip.

Out-of-This-World Stone Paperweights

What You Need

large smooth stones
scrap paper
pencil
acrylic paints and paintbrushes
newspaper (to work on)

What You Do

1. Tell children they will be making Dad a Father's Day gift that is "out of this world!"

2. Make sure the stone is a good size for a paperweight and that it has a smooth, flat surface for painting. Wash and air-dry the stone.

3. Sketch a "spacey" idea on a piece of scrap paper: a spaceship, a Martian, the planets, the stars, the sun, or the moon.

4. Use acrylics to paint the image on a stone. If desired, the entire surface may first be painted a background color, such as a pale blue. After the initial coat dries, a large yellow crescent moon can be added. Or a multicolored background of fiery reds and oranges can host the shape of a silver spaceship. Allow the stone to dry thoroughly.

5. Children can also make Out-of-This-World Stone Paperweights for their desks at school.

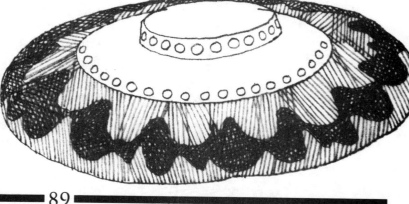

Stone 'n' Shell Figures

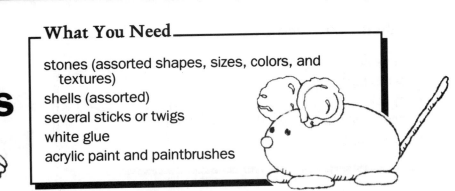

What You Need

stones (assorted shapes, sizes, colors, and textures)

shells (assorted)

several sticks or twigs

white glue

acrylic paint and paintbrushes

What You Do

1. Here's a suggestion for making a stone figure. Use two medium-sized flat stones for the feet. Spread some glue on the top of each stone. Add a large round stone for the body. Make sure the body stone balances on the feet stones. If necessary, prop the body stone with other stones to hold it in place while it dries. Allow the glue to dry completely (it may take a while) before adding another stone.

2. Dab some glue on top of the body stone and attach a smaller round stone for the head. Let the glue dry. Glue long sticks onto the body for the arms. Tiny pebbles or pieces of shells may be glued onto the head for facial features. Or paint on facial features with acrylic paint.

3. Once kids have the basics, they can let their imaginations come into play. For example, they can glue a shell hat to the figure's head or attach a scallop shell to the top of a stick for an umbrella.

4. Stone 'n' Shell animals are also delightful to make. First, think about the animal's shape. Then find shells that represent the animal's coloring.

5. For a penguin, glue two small feet stones to a rock base. Use a pair of mussel shells for flippers. Fit them onto an oval-shaped white body stone. Add painted eyes to a small stone head. The contrast makes for an interesting figure. When making the penguin, children will contrast light-colored stones with dark shells. They can also contrast a rough body with smooth-shell flippers.

6. Children can create other animals, keeping in mind the coloring, texture, size, and shape of the animal's body. Tell them not to leave a stone unturned!

What You Need

any natural objects found at the beach (shells, from horseshoe crabs to periwinkles; seaweed; pebbles; dried starfish; and so on)

large piece of driftwood or other interestingly shaped piece of wood (for base)

white glue

rag

Beach Find Sculptures

What You Do

1. Tell children that the seashore is a tremendous treasure chest of shells and other ''natural'' objects that can be used for sculptures.

2. Thoroughly soak and air-dry (in a sunny place) all the ''beach finds.''

3. Arrange the shells, seaweed, pebbles, and other ''finds'' on a big piece of driftwood or other wood base. Select large, colorful shells as a focal point and build up the design by adding smaller shells and other beach finds. Experiment by turning the objects in different ways to find good positions and places on the wood where they seem to ''fit.'' A piece of seaweed, for example, may be draped over a pointy section of the wood.

4. Glue each piece into place on the wooden base. Use only the amount of glue needed to make each part stick. Any excess glue can be wiped off with a damp rag.

5. Turn the sculpture and view it from all sides. Add any other shells, stones, or seaweed, until it seems finished.

6. When children look at their Beach Find Sculptures, they'll be reminded of the wonderful treasures they can find at the beach.

Sand Casts

Hand Sand Cast and Sandy Animal Track Cast

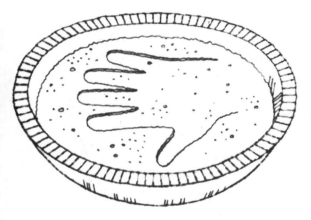

newspaper (to work on)

8-inch (20-cm) aluminum foil pie plate (for hand cast)

sand (to fill plate)

cornstarch

1 cup (250 ml) water (at room temperature)

2 cups (500 ml) plaster of Paris

spoon

disposable plastic container or large can (to hold plaster mixture)

cardboard (for animal track cast)

masking tape (for animal track cast)

Safety Note: Read and follow warnings on container. Plaster creates dust. Do not cast any body parts because plaster can cause serious burns. Teacher should mix plaster outdoors or in a separate ventilated area.

What You Do

Tell children that casting is a process for making a copy of a 3-dimensional object or shape. A cast is formed in a mold by using a plaster substance and letting it harden. The copy has the form and detail of the original.

Hand Sand Cast

1. Spread out some newspaper sheets to work on. Fill the pie plate with sand, leaving about 1/2 inch (1 1/4 cm) of space at the top. Add some water to make the sand firm but not too wet. Press a child's entire hand flat down into the sand to make a handprint.

2. Sprinkle cornstarch over the print. Completely cover it and the area around it with a thin layer. The cornstarch keeps the sand from sticking to the plaster.

3. Pour 1 cup (250 ml) water into a container. (Teacher should add 2 cups (500 ml) plaster of Paris to the water. Mix together, stirring until the mixture is smooth and feels about as thick as melted ice cream. If the mixture is not thick enough, add a little more plaster.)

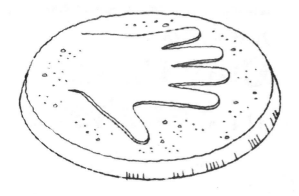

4. Using a spoon, children can carefully add the plaster of Paris to the handprint, filling in all areas of the print. Then spoon, or slowly pour, the rest of the plaster of Paris over the remaining sand. Add it evenly over the entire surface, using up all of the mixture.

5. Wipe the spoon immediately and put aside the empty container for disposal. Never pour plaster of Paris down the sink drain because it will harden and clog the pipes.

6. Let the plaster of Paris cast harden for one hour. Remove the cast from the pie plate. Turn the cast over to see a plaster cast of the hand.

7. There will probably be some sand around the handprint. Do not remove the sand yet. Place the cast on a sheet of newspaper and allow it to dry overnight or longer. When the Hand Sand Cast is completely dry, brush off some of the sand or leave it for a textured effect.

Sandy Animal Track Cast

1. If you feel adventurous, take the class outdoors to make casts of animal tracks. Or give them directions for making these casts on an outing with their families.

2. For each cast, use a sheet of cardboard instead of a pie plate. When an animal track is found, roll the cardboard into a cylinder big enough to surround the track. Tape the rolled cardboard and press it into the earth.

3. Follow the same steps as before, starting with sprinkling the cornstarch. When the plaster of Paris dries, lift out the Sandy Animal Track Cast and peel away the cardboard.

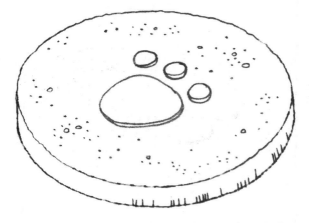

Clay Casts of Seashells

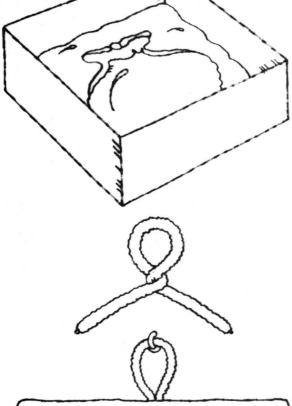

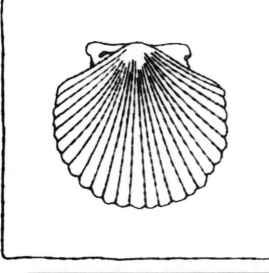

What You Need

newspaper (to work on)

soft, nonhardening clay (modeling clay)

small cardboard or plastic container (about 3 inches (7 1/2 cm) deep and wide enough for the size of the mold wanted)

shells

1 cup (250 ml) water at room temperature

2 cups (500 ml) plaster of Paris

spoon

disposable plastic container or large tin can (to hold plaster mixture)

pipe cleaners

Safety Note: Read and follow warnings on container. Plaster creates dust. Do not cast any body parts because plaster can cause serious burns. Teacher should mix plaster outdoors or in a separate ventilated area.

What You Do

1. Press softened clay into the bottom of a small container so that it's flat. The clay should be about 1 inch (2 1/2 cm) thick all around.

2. Press a shell (or several shells) into the clay deeply enough to make an imprint that will show the texture and the whole shape. Remove the shell(s).

3. Teacher should prepare the plaster of Paris mixture. (Refer to directions on pages 92–93.) The proportions given will yield enough mixture for about three shell casts in small containers. Carefully spoon about 1/2 inch (1 1/4 cm) of the plaster of Paris mixture on top of the clay.

4. Cut a 5-inch (12½-cm) piece of pipe cleaner. Make it into a loop with both ends sticking out as shown. Twist the base of the loop once. Stick both ends of the pipe cleaner into the plaster mixture, positioning it near one edge. The entire loop should stick out. This loop will later be used for hanging the cast.

5. Let the plaster harden overnight. Teacher or another adult should cut open the container and ease or pop out the plaster cast. Children can now peel off the clay. The cast is a *reverse* imprint.

What You Need

6 small paper cups
sand
water
food coloring
6 spoons
newspaper (for working on and drying sand)
empty wooden box (such as a cigar box)
white glue and small brush

Sand Painting
Sunny Sandbox

Sand painting is an art highly developed by the Navajo Nation. Artists dribble colorful sand through their fingers to make beautiful pictures. Here's an idea for a sand painting you can make to capture the summertime feeling of sun and sand.

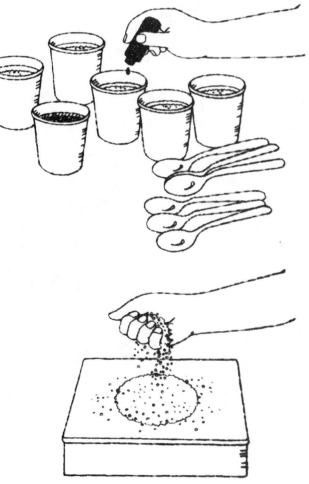

What You Do

1. Color the sand by filling each cup halfway with sand. Add water until it completely covers the sand. To each cup, add drops of food coloring. You can make each cup of sand a different color. You can also make different shades of one color. (If you use only a few drops of food coloring, the shade will be lighter. If you add more drops of coloring, the shade will be darker.) Stir the sand, water, and food coloring in each cup. Let the mixture stand for about fifteen minutes.

2. Pour out the extra water. Spoon each color or shade of sand onto a separate sheet of newspaper. Spread the sand out to dry.

3. Let the box top be your "canvas" and the dry sand be your "paint." With a brush and glue, "sketch" all the parts of a smiling sun that you want to be one color. Let the colorful sand run through your fingers onto the area that you brushed with glue. Gently blow off the excess sand. Continue working in this way with other colors, until the sun is shimmering with sand.

4. "Paint" the remainder of the box top with sand. You might make bands of colors streaking from the sun across the lid—ribbons of orange, red, and purple. Or you might show the brightness of the sun against a pale blue sky.

5. Let the glued sand dry completely. Then fill your Sunny Sandbox with special things. Let the sun shine!

Sandy Jar Candlesticks

Glass is made by melting a mixture of sand, soda (not the kind you drink), and lime (not the kind you eat). Recycle a glass jar into a candlestick. Then use sand (one of the things used to make glass) to decorate the jar.

What You Need

sand
6 small paper cups
food coloring
6 spoons
newspaper (for drying sand)
a short glass jar
candle (taller than the jar)
matches *for adult*

What You Do

1. Color the sand as you did for the sand painting. Fill each cup half-full with sand. Add water to cover it. Then add drops of food coloring. After 15 minutes, pour out the extra water. Spoon each color of sand onto a separate sheet of newspaper. Spread it out to dry. Dry and save the cups.

2. Ask an adult to light the candle and drip some wax into the bottom center of the jar.

3. Blow out the candle. While the wax is still warm, press the bottom of the candle onto the drippings. Make sure the wax holds the candle in place.

4. Use one of the cups you saved to scoop up one color of sand. (Make sure the sand is completely dry!) Pour the sand around the candle. Add a layer of another color. Keep adding colored layers until the sand is about 1 inch (2 1/2 cm) from the top of the jar. (It's okay if it doesn't reach that high.)

5. Set your Sandy Jar Candlestick on your dining-room table at home. Have a deLIGHTful dinner!

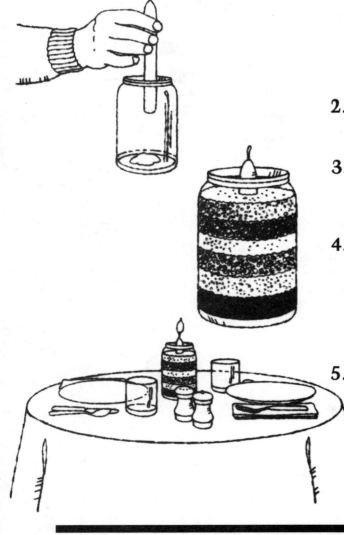